Malcolm Nabarro

From Mozart
to the Med

...a new life afloat

a **LOCKSIDE** imprint [07]

Published by Lulu in 2007

ISBN 978-1-84799-217-8

The extract from 'The East Coast' by Derek Bowskill is reproduced
with the kind permission of publisher Imray Laurie Norie & Wilson

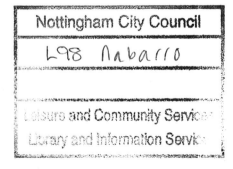
ii

To Emma and Benjamin
...and those that follow!

Introduction

This is my story of a crisis that turned into an opportunity.

I hesitate to use the word, crisis. We have a family policy of approaching all problematic or challenging moments by asking "is it terminal?" It usually isn't of course but we find it helps place stressful moments in some kind of context. This time asking the question didn't help. It felt as though it *was* terminal, it felt like a bereavement, it felt how it must feel to lose a child or a spouse.

It wasn't the first time I needed to stop and re-evaluate. For ten years after leaving music college I worked as an instrumental teacher but I also spent those ten years trying to escape from it, to pursue what I really needed to do, which was perform. As a musician it's impossible to separate career from everyday existence and if things aren't going well with the career it can make for a very unhappy life. I 'engineered' a way out of my dilemma, a way to take us forward. Complete with mortgage, two young children and a wife fantastically supportive I resigned from a secure, pensionable teaching post and overnight became a free-lance conductor. Despite reservations from some quarters it worked. We survived financially but more importantly and I'm sure Janet would agree, we grew as people and musicians.

This earlier experience, a real step into the unknown, taught me a great deal and probably helped enormously when years later I was faced with a crisis of far greater magnitude, one that took us both to the edge. There is no doubt I'd learnt that life is not a rehearsal. If the future looks bleak, unsure, then take another route. That route might lead to the unexpected, mine certainly did, but then fate does play a part. Fate brought Janet and me together when we were very young, how could I not trust in it?

A note on the name *'Starry Vere'*

We renamed the boat not long after we bought her, which is supposed to be unlucky among mariners. The name we chose, *'Starry Vere'* comes from the opera **Billy Budd** by Benjamin Britten. In turn Britten was inspired by Herman Mellville's last novel, **'Billy Budd, Sailor'.**

This is not just a favourite opera of mine but one that is full of meaning on many levels. The story is set in the British Navy of the late 18th century. Starry Vere is the nickname given to Captain Fairfax Vere by his adoring crew. In book and opera he is portrayed as a truly outstanding captain, compassionate, fair and sensitive, a man of action whose recreation is literature. Aboard his ship Indomitable, the Master at Arms, John Glaggert, the embodiment of evil falsely accuses an impressed sailor, Billy Budd, handsome, innocent, a force for good amongst his shipmates, of mutiny. Billy's only flaw is a stammer and when under the stress of Claggert's accusation, in the presence of Captain Vere and unable to articulate a defence, he lashes out and kills Claggert. Billy must be condemned to hang by his fatherly but just captain on whom is laid the burden of perceiving the truth, the conflict between good and evil, yet his allegiance can only be to discipline.

I find the music immensely moving and the story both poignant and inspiring.

This 'tis to have been from the first
In a domestic heaven nursed,
Under the discipline severe
Of Fairfax and the starry Vere.
Marvell

Starry Vere on the canal du Midi near Beziers

1

.... a glimpse of a possibility

It was August and unusually hot. Janet and I emerged from the busy concourse of London's Charing Cross station, blinking into the sudden glare of a bright mid-summer sun, still high even though the afternoon was moving toward evening. We eased our way through the crowded pavement; a congestion of locals, moving at pace with knowledgeable determination and tourists, less sure, idling, dawdling even, with all the time in the world. So much to negotiate, a distinctive jam of London traffic, busy black cabs, red open-top tourist buses and urgent messenger motorbikes; a shock to us after weeks of solitude. Crossing The Strand we joined the crowds snaking to and from Trafalgar Square, our aim the historic church of St Martin's in the Fields where our musician son Benjamin would be performing that evening. It was busy, absolutely throbbing, right at the peak of the tourist season but the church offered sanctuary, a peaceful coolness and the wonderful sound of music.

Arriving in the centre of London by train was not how it was meant to be. We had taken a little over a month to reach the capital, normally a modest three-hour car journey by motorway from our native Nottingham, but this time was not normal, we had departed by boat, set on enjoying a leisurely trip down the east coast of England. No, our plan was to reach the capital in style, cruising up the Thames in *Starry Vere* and to 'lie in state' in St.Catherine Dock marina, wonderfully adjacent to Tower Bridge and giving us by far the cheapest bed in central London. Remarkably our sea passages had not been hindered by bad weather but now it seemed our good fortune had ended. With a weather forecast for the Thames estuary predicting high winds, prudently, reluctantly, we left *Starry Vere* moored on the River Medway at Rochester and let the train take the strain.

On reflection our day in London was far more significant than either Janet or I appreciated. So much had passed in preparation for departure to our new life, but so much was still to come in fulfilling a dream. London was certainly not the beginning of the story but it was a pivotal moment, a brief and very poignant reminder of the life from which we were journeying. The feelings we experienced during a marvellous concert were sharpened by the central involvement of Ben, who's growing maturity as a musician was very evident. But it was the music that cast its usual spell; Wolfgang Amadeus Mozart, some would say the greatest composer ever and certainly the most naturally gifted genius. His music is direct, if you are receptive there is no stopping its impact. With our son a wonderful and sensitive soloist in the G major Violin Concerto, we experienced double the impact, double the emotion.

And that life from which we were journeying? As professional musicians we had been totally engrossed in a passion. For over fifteen years life had revolved around the professional orchestra I had founded and conducted. Guiding its growth from just an idea to an important regional artistic resource had been hard work yet exciting. A management team developed, complementing artistic progress and eventually, with my complete acquiescence, control passed to a board of directors charged with the continuing health and development of the organisation. All worked well for a number of years but relationships slowly deteriorated and the best way I can describe the net effect is an organisation becoming poisoned. A variety of forces were at work but the end result felt like a devastating betrayal. The pure enjoyment of making music was being suffocated by intense unhappiness and stress, to the point where I realised to continue would be emotionally and even physically damaging. Even if I had battled on I was sure my career would be professionally impoverished. I had fought passionately to maintain the values I believed were true for an arts organisation but the writing was on the wall and although intensely painful, I just knew it was time to get out.

Performing great music is both a privilege and a tremendous burden. The feelings can be narcotic, those of wonder and elation, of satisfaction and awe. I found myself in the public eye, to varying degrees and particularly as a conductor a certain amount of status is bestowed, whether one courts it or not. Loss of status, of personal worth, of a job indeed, is debilitating. It was also particularly tough for Janet because she played in the orchestra, she experienced the growing problems from all sides and it was only a matter of time before it became emotionally untenable for her to continue. It was certainly a traumatic time, a bereavement.

Five years later, the London concert was the beginning of the end of that particular painful voyage. Both our son and daughter are destined to be successful musicians so we feel easy that through family connections we will still be in contact with the profession. We can understand and enjoy the highs and lows Emma and Benjamin will experience and by association we will feel them too. It was a symbolic underlining of the past, the moment when it really registered we were moving on to the adventure of a new life.

How we got from that situation to buying and restoring a classic boat and then to hatch the crazy plan to sail off into the sunset, is still a mystery - particularly when your wife can't even swim! There has to be a spiritual element, not religious but a guiding force leading us in the direction we took. We had never owned a boat or collectively even considered owning one. Certainly since teenage years I had been fascinated by sea adventures, avidly reading accounts of such epic tales as Sir Francis Chichester's round the world voyage or the fascinating account of the Kontiki Expedition. As a young student, finding Nicholas Monsarrat's classic war-time novel *The Cruel Sea* set as an English literature examination course book made the difference between passing and failing!

A very good friend from Nottingham, fellow musician and collaborator *extraordinaire*, Brian Wilson, with wife Sue, had invested in a small boat, a day cruiser, giving them both the chance to escape onto the local waterways, a way of releasing the pressures of life. It must have been June or July, not long after my break with the orchestra, when Janet and I were invited to spend a day on the river. I remember it vividly. The weather was gorgeous and armed with a few bottles of bubbly we joined Brian and Sue at a local marina. Why I remember it so vividly was the shock and yes, it was a shock, that everyone on the river, the other boat owners, were amazingly friendly. Over the past couple of years I had become so cynical and introspective that just a mere wave, a cheerful good morning, from people without hang ups, hidden agendas, or axes to grind, was the most amazing eye opener, a revelation, a glimpse of a possibility. Brian has much to answer for! Later, on reflection, the ideas welling up seemed out of the question, unobtainable, unreasonable even, and all such thoughts were suppressed. As it transpired only temporarily, the genie was well and truly out of the bottle and refused to be put back.

In August we took a short camping holiday on Shell Island, overlooking Cardigan Bay in North Wales. This was the defining moment. The weather was bright and sunny and as I watched the boats come and go from a nearby marina the sense of freedom, of escape, was amazingly therapeutic and empowering; the moment when my zest for life was re-ignited and, as they say, the rest is history. I returned from the Shell Island holiday fired with the prospect of looking for a boat.

Janet? Poor long suffering Janet. She must have been bracing herself for another roller-coaster ride but at least I was alive, motivated and quite likely improving company. But how does one start and how would we pay for it? Janet was still working but technically I was out of a job, just the time to make a large capital outlay! Undaunted I began searching through the boating press, the many glossy magazines, crammed full of information, with vessels for sale of every shape and size. Living close to the River Trent we recollected seeing boats near the main road into Newark. This proved to be Newark Marina and I dragged the whole family along for our first opportunity to clamber aboard a selection of motor cruisers and to gauge the prices. Oh dear, the prices. We soon realised a mortgage would be required for anything decent. We also quickly realised many motor cruisers have the feel of a caravan inside. I was looking for a boat, no a ship, certainly something with the salty character of a real vessel. There was one, an American style trawler yacht called *French Leave*. She grabbed us all but thankfully turned out to be already sold, saving us from a financial investment well beyond our reach.

It was crazy. I knew nothing about boats, I didn't even know anyone who owned one other than Brian. Fibreglass, wood, steel, motor, sail, there are so many choices, so many potential areas to come unstuck, especially when serious money is at stake. I remained undaunted, the stubborn streak prevailed, and then a boat jumped off the page of a brokerage magazine and presented itself to me. There wasn't even a picture, just a description of a forty-two foot, steel and timber vessel, lying in the east coast port of Ipswich and at a price we might just be able to afford. It was time to be bold and a viewing was arranged.

We drew up on the quayside at Neptune Marine, virtually adjacent to a classic looking boat with white hull, varnished wooden superstructure and a couple of masts adding to the attractive lines. It looked like a serious vessel, could it be the one?
I was smitten with love at first sight… for the second time in my life!

She was named *Mailoma*, which we disliked from the start. The association with 'melanoma' was unpleasant, but we had to chuckle when the broker, in response to voicing our dislike of the name, suggested it would grow on us. Although, amongst the marine fraternity, changing the name of a boat is supposed to bring nothing but bad luck, if we purchased that name just had to be changed.

I knew immediately we would buy her but although completely captivated there was room for negotiation and we dragged ourselves away from Ipswich leaving the broker charged to relay our offer to the owner. *Mailoma* had evidently been on the market for some time, yet the owner's reluctance to negotiate resulted in a sticky period when the broker had to work very hard to clinch the deal. But a deal was indeed done and the night after I dropped an envelope containing the deposit cheque into the mailbox proved a sleepless one.

What had I done? What on earth was I doing?

As I discovered, it was usual form for the purchase to be 'subject to survey' and on the appointed day I drove down to Ipswich to see the boat out of the water and to meet the surveyor. Janet was working but our daughter Emma came for the ride. Arriving back at Neptune Marine *Mailoma* was now suspended high and dry in the travel lift ready for our inspection. She looked enormous, very impressive with two large propellers, at least I recognised those but I wasn't sure about the other bits and bobs. Such was my excitement I introduced Emma to the assembled group as my wife! Pretty, blond and sixteen, for a moment I was the envy of all, apart from Emma of course, who was mortified; such an embarrassment, dad was really losing it this time.

A ladder was produced to climb on board and we spent a goodly time inspecting and discovering. The surveyor, a local man who purported to know the boat well, was very helpful and at the time I thought he even-handedly pointed out the problems, potential problems and merits. I haven't dwelt on the implications, there is no real point, but although his subsequent written report seemed comprehensive and balanced it was only later, during the years of renovation, it became clear how much he had missed, or refrained from including. I have often speculated, particularly at low points, that if I had been aware of the complete picture would I have still made the purchase, would I have been frightened off?

It's a difficult one. The enormous challenge of refurbishing and renovating did present me with a unique opportunity to acquire so many new skills, surely indispensable for successful and safe living-aboard. There is no doubt I now know the boat inside out but the financial cost in bringing her up to a modern and safe sea-worthy standard has been considerable. Perhaps on this occasion ignorance was bliss, even essential… part of the scheme of things. The boat was destined to be ours, warts and all.

So, vessel purchased, this is the story of our 'voyage'. We have no dramatic tales of ocean crossings, for our voyaging rarely took us out of sight of land. We have no encounters with waves as high as houses, or exotic sea creatures, or pirates. What we are able to relate though would have been hard to imagine. Situations and people, dramas, adventures, high and low points. We were to be blessed with the most fantastic experiences as we departed a life musical and journeyed to one equally challenging but distinctly nautical.

And simmering gently on the bottom shelf of my consciousness the personal sub-voyage of rediscovery, of simply relishing a reason to keep going, of having found that all important challenge. It was, quite simply, a crucial step along the therapeutic road to recovery of self-esteem.

2

…a spot of welding or a little gentle re-wiring

In very pleasant sunshine, late in the first June of the new millennium, we made our final preparations to bid farewell to Farndon Marina. For the past four years Janet and I had worked toward embarking on one of life's last great escapes. Four years of planning, of doubting, dreaming and worrying but most of all four years of labour as we renovated and rebuilt our classic motor cruiser *Starry Vere*.

Farndon Marina, or as we affectionately prefer Farndon *'aarrbour* (imagine our man o' the sea Norfolk accent) is a perfect sanctuary off the River Trent, just above the historic town of Newark in Nottinghamshire. Set in what appears to be wonderful parkland, it has literally been carved out of a number of exhausted gravel pits by the Ainsworth family who had spent their lives working and living on the Trent. Originally it did bear the name 'Harbour' but pandering to modern marketing it has succumbed to 'Marina'. Husband and father Mark Ainsworth is now in semi-retirement but the harbour is still a family run business with son Paul managing. It was a visionary move by Mark and the family have to be admired for what has been created and for their continuing energy in improving and developing the moorings. But to call it a marina is a misnomer. It has the working feel of a harbour and during our four years in residence *Starry Vere* was virtually rebuilt, with more time spent on the hard than in the water. No matter, whether marina or harbour it boasts an asset that raises its status high above any other mooring we have ever found, a superb toilet block with showers to die for!

Starry Vere bears the marque Sealion 42, and although I didn't realise at the time of purchase she was in her unaltered and original state. In the early 1960's J G Meakes of Marlow on Thames were importing steel hulls from Holland and fitting them out in a very classic British style with one eye looking back to the traditions of earlier times. Constructed in 1964, an extraordinary amount of beautiful hardwood had been used on the decking, superstructure and in the main saloon and aft cabin, the master cabin. Separate single berths here, after all it was described as a 'gentleman's motor yacht'. Interestingly there was a concession to the fashions of the swinging 60's; the abundant use of the new wonder surface, Formica. The galley in particular was finished in a fetching grey and white check. We joked the boat had an 'upstairs-downstairs' feel. Lavish wood furniture for the gentleman skipper but in the forward crew area, in the galley, heads and bow cabin, functional wall-to-wall cold Formica.

For the first year or so the engine room was a black hole, into which I ventured with nothing but apprehension. But then this was my first boat. I had no idea what to expect, no idea what was normal or what was a problem, even what was serious. Fired with enthusiasm I just set about using my initiative and read every relevant book I could lay hands on; launching myself onto a massive learning curve. It quickly became all embracing, wonderfully stimulating and often very scary, even when the boat was safely tied up, which it certainly remained for the first couple of months.

Lifting the cabin floor revealed a matched parallel-lying pair of large elderly engines. Now forgive me if I wax lyrical about these engines, I have noticed many a family member's eyes glaze over when I launch forth on this subject but the more I become acquainted with their pedigree the more I become fascinated, to the point of being quite proud and protective of them. They are very interesting, with an unusual experimental design. Information is now quite scarce but their origin was probably American in concept and developed in Britain in the 60's under the Rootes Company name. They were actually manufactured by the engineering company, Tillet and Stevens, in Maidstone, Kent. The engine block has three cylinders, each containing two horizontally opposed pistons, meaning there are no valves, so for fuel injection and exhaust abstraction they rely on a two-stroke cycle. Sadly they are now entirely obsolete but being so heavily built (the handbook describing them as industrial engines) and particularly used in a boat installation, where the use is far lighter than road transport, they should keep *Starry Vere* powered for a while yet.

Electrically the boat was in the Stone Age. I suppose in the 60's expectations where somewhat different. No navigation electronics, no electric toilet, no microwave? These are certainly not luxury items these days and as a live-a-board boat we demand all home comforts and now even boast a scaled down version of a domestic front loading all singing and dancing washing machine. But having only a very basic knowledge about the mystery of electricity it was necessary to go on reading. What became worryingly clear was that the boat had been wired in what these days could be considered a very crude fashion. The more I read the more I became paranoid. The best book to really put the frighteners on any steel boat owner is 'Metal Corrosion in Steel Boats' by Nigel Warren … and I read it, cover to cover! Emma described it at the time, in her usual dry understatement, as her father's light bedtime reading. This is a splendid and immensely informative textbook but on first reading there seemed no future for Starry Vere, she would surely rot away. Without doubt this book should come with a health warning!

A complete rewiring seemed the only alternative and I am proud to say, with some professional advice and a considerable financial investment, ("as normal", I can hear Janet saying) the boat is now electrically state of the art.

The refit was certainly comprehensive. Out went the Formica clad galley, with the enamelled Baby Belling cooker; all was gutted and rebuilt with gas and plumbing systems renewed. Out went the single bunks in the aft cabin, again gutted and rebuilt complete with double bed and en-suite facilities, including electric toilet.

Lifting the entire deck was certainly one of my major challenges. The teak had been laid on ply, which in turn had been bolted onto the steel hull. Over the years water had ingressed and now obvious signs of corrosion were becoming a problem. I balked at this task for some time but finally it had to be tackled and hundreds of pieces of teak were lifted and catalogued on a master plan, like an enormous jigsaw puzzle. The deck was then shot blasted, painted with epoxy and new ply bolted down to form a bed for the teak. Janet skilfully made large templates from rolls of old wallpaper to ensure the ply was accurately cut to fit the shape of the deck. It was like an enormous dress pattern. Every piece of the precious teak was refurbished before being re-laid. I can't imagine what it would have cost to replace those wonderful three-quarter inch thick nuggets of gold, even if a source could be found. But it was done and new stainless steel stanchions supporting the solid teak rail provided the icing on the cake. She looked pretty smart.

The day for which we had worked so hard had finally become a reality and thankfully our mid-week departure meant there were only a couple of harbour staff around. We took on fuel and without witness or ceremony *Starry Vere* slipped out into the river's familiar flow for a final time. This is not to say we were creeping out in anonymous fashion. We had made so many friends in the harbour and our future plans and constant travail on the boat were a source of fascination among fellow boaters. So much so that at weekends it was difficult to make progress as a stream of passing folk chatted, examined and freely offered advice and assistance. We enjoyed the camaraderie enormously and I thrived on the advice as a new skill was tackled, such as a spot of welding or a little gentle re-wiring. I became an avid brain picker but what grew to be irritating was the jolly person who came along, stood back, surveyed the project and could only find to say, "you've got a big job on there mate", and there were many! No, we had a heavy social life at Farndon and before our departure we threw a farewell party onboard a fully flagged and lit *Starry Vere*.

We were now glad to be leaving quietly. It was a thoughtful moment. Family, friends, careers left behind, out into the unknown, it was best to be alone. And so, heading north, which confusingly one does to go *down* the Trent, we began our voyage to the sea.

Initially it seemed a preamble, a prelude, a finding out if the boat and we were up to it. We had to remind ourselves it was for real as the familiarity of the territory gave it just another summer holiday feel. The river winds through flat yet attractive agricultural land, rich in bird-life. Janet and I had walked the same riverbank on so many occasions, in all seasons and in all weathers, spotting intent wading grey herons concentrating on a next meal in the shallows and the more energetic ever busy diving black cormorants, happier out in the faster deeper water. In early summer, looking to our right over the fields of ripening corn or fluorescent yellow rape, the larks ascending, singing, then rapidly falling, never failed to remind us of the evocative music of Vaughan Williams. He really got it so right. And in the trees and bushes blackbirds, producing a virtuoso range of song that we have never heard matched. We cruised past the river's 'genuine' marina, the definitely upwardly mobile Newark Marina, which specialises in selling large and expensive plastic boats. Then into the built-up area, past desirable flats and apartments created from the old riverside warehouses and so popular with large numbers of commuters plying the fast, or maybe not so fast, East Coast railway down to the capital. Through Town lock, alongside the towering lichen clad ancient walls of Newark Castle. Through the narrow demanding grey stone arch of the old road bridge. Past a scruffier industrial riverside area, complete with scrap-yard trying hard with derelict fences to restrain piles of beaten and forgotten cars from tumbling into the water. Then, once through Nether lock, out into the last of the pleasant north Nottinghamshire countryside.

The river was empty this fine evening and we reached the sea lock at Cromwell just about at high water, ideal to take us on the ebb to our mooring for the night at Torksey, the cut off the river giving access to the ancient Fossdyke navigation stretching to Lincoln and beyond. Every time we moor at Torksey we are reminded of that fateful day in late August a couple of years before, when we woke to hear of the unfolding tragedy in a Paris underpass. Later the same day, as we locked through at Cromwell, we had found the young lady lock keeper in the control room glued to her TV, unable, like most of the nation, to believe the breaking news of Princess Diana's tragic death. Torksey is an interesting and historic place but for one reason or another our arrival on the excellent mooring was always coloured by some drama or excitement.

Like my very first encounter with Torksey, arriving from downstream, after dark, in late January 1996. It was just after *Starry Vere* (still bearing that awful name *Mailoma*) had been purchased and the culmination of a second attempt to sail her up the coast from Ipswich. It would have been far too easy, apart from far too expensive, to have popped the boat on the back of a lorry and have her delivered to a mooring in Lincoln. But where's the fun in that? Sailing her down the River Orwell, up the East Anglian coast, crossing The Wash and into the Humber estuary offered the chance to embark on the great learning curve for real. Of course at that time I hadn't a clue, so a professional skipper was enlisted, along with two other experienced crew. We had made an initial attempt the previous November but this was aborted due to bad weather. It hadn't stopped us taking the opportunity of navigating down the beautiful Orwell, just out beyond Harwich, where I experienced a first taste of bad weather in the open sea... in a small boat. On that occasion we made the prudent decision to about turn, back into the sanctuary of the river and to a safe mooring at Pin Mill. Our reward was a fantastic seafarers evening in the famous Butt and Oyster Inn, complete with log fire, beer from the barrel and salty anecdotes. This boating business began to look like fun. Bad weather persisted and the following day we had no choice but to leave *Mailoma* on her mooring in Ipswich and return to the real world of working for a living.

It was the following January before we had another weather and work window but our second attempt to leave Ipswich wasn't without incident either. A misunderstanding over lock opening times as we headed for a morning departure from the historic dock brought us to an abrupt halt. The lock only operates for a few minutes either side of high tide and we had missed this small window of opportunity. Twelve hours now had to pass before the next high tide would allow those lock gates to open again; twelve hours for four dubious characters topped out in SAS type woolly hats, to stalk around damp and chilly Ipswich, killing time. With window shopping exhausted we resorted to a couple of hours in a disquietingly empty cinema watching the latest James Bond spectacular and then far too long in a 'greasy spoon' café suffering an all-day breakfast ... at four in the afternoon.

High tide was around nine o'clock in the evening and so it was in complete darkness when we slipped our lines, passed through the offending lock and gingerly, oh so gingerly, picked our way down the Orwell. Navigating the buoyed channel, flashing greens on our port side, reds to starboard, we aimed to avoid the many rows of moored yachts and their unlit mooring buoys. A couple of hours it took and as the river began to noticeably widen we were hindered by the unhelpful mosaic created by all manner of shore-side lighting as we strained to pick out the navigation lights of a cross channel ferry heading into Harwich, or was it heading out? The increasing movement underfoot was a sure sign we were leaving the calmness of the river and emerging into the North Sea. With a turn to port and the adoption of a northerly course we began to trace the line of the east coast, heading for the Humber estuary that would eventually give us access to the River Trent. Life was certainly taking on a change!

On reflection the skipper chose to progress at a very cautious pace because it was after some twenty-four hours of continuous cruising, sharing out the watch in true nautical fashion, before we anchored in the Humber. Now, not to criticise an experienced skipper but I am still not sure why we tolerated a most uncomfortable twelve hours at anchor in the estuary, a pretty grim place at the best of times, when we could have nipped into Hull marina with the prospect of a pint and a comfortable sleep. At the time I had no idea what the alternatives were and so was in no position to question but the roll of the boat was mind numbing. I experienced a first bout of seasickness and certainly couldn't share the passion of my fellow crew for bacon sandwiches, at all hours and at all states of the sea. I guess it was all part of the induction.

The following morning dawned grey and cold but tides dictated we couldn't escape the incessant rolling until about eleven. Our progress even then was very tentative, following the buoyed channel of the estuary and into the mouth of the Trent at the infamous Trent Falls. The days are short in January and dusk fell with us still making our way upstream. Four salty characters, wrapped up against the cold, speeding up the river on a spring flood, the boat's spotlight picking out the twists and turns just in time. I'm surprised we didn't attract the attention of the authorities.

In the thickening gloom we were searching for a left turn, a turn to port, taking us off the main river into Torksey cut. Using the spotlight and hand torches, creeping forward as slow as we dare to maintain steerage in the last of the flood, we scoured the bank-side, straining for that watery gap. The relief at spotting the junction was short lived and gave way to a moment of panic as, halfway turned into the cut, a shout from the outside helm reported a problem with the port gear control, there was *no* control, the port engine couldn't be disengaged and so negating the effect of the rudder being turned to port. We were heading into the blackness toward where the riverbank would be for sure. Fortunately, during my many earlier explorations of *Starry Vere's* gear, I had noted that the inside helm controls were independent and so tumbling into the saloon I was able to disengage the port side drive. Later we found it was only a split pin that had jumped out rather than a cable failure but drama to the end, excitement that we could have well done without.

We moored to the deserted wooden floating pontoons, by now glistening with a layer of light frost and after a little investigation marched the half mile to the recommended Hulme Arms. It was a Saturday evening and this particular hostelry was obviously a popular, reasonably smart, pub and eating-house. As for us, we had arrived from the sea; unshaven, uncaring, a pint and a good meal was our just reward. Returning to the boat that night I slept probably the best sleep I have ever experienced. Amazingly tired yet wonderfully content and satisfied.

Six years later, with the June evening peacefully drawing in, we nudged alongside those same wooden pontoons without drama or crisis. A wander down to the Hulme Arms for old times sake and then we turned in for our first night as true live-a-boards.

Janet enjoying breakfast on the aft deck

3

...you can't push-start a boat!

From Torksey to Trent Falls, where the river spills out into the Humber, is the difficult bit. Although the estuary is still some thirty-six miles away, the effect of its enormous tidal range now demands attention. Any mariner aiming for the sea has to give it due consideration and reflect on the options available for ensuring there is water under the keel. Timing then is crucial and although we have successfully negotiated the river a number of times we still labour over tide tables and charts to ensure we've got it right. This is probably because the very first time, despite a year of night school navigation classes, with certificates to prove it... we didn't!

We were moored in Lincoln that first year and this was to be our inaugural summer holiday afloat. The straight and narrow Fosse Dyke was the first waterway to negotiate and this I found a surprisingly tiring operation, demanding sustained concentration just to steer the boat in a straight line for such a length of time. But successfully completed we were able to enjoy mooring once again at Torksey for the night. A new electric fridge had just been fitted in the still Formica clad galley but although I had no idea at the time, the ancient dynamos fitted on the engines for battery charging were far from adequate, particularly at the relatively slow speed necessary on inland waterways. Consequently, the following day when I went to fire up the engines with a view to leaving Torksey at our carefully calculated departure time, the batteries were well and truly flat. With hindsight of course, plus the knowledge gained from my ever growing nautical library, I now know it is good practice to have separate batteries for engine starting but at the time, I didn't. Plus, alas, the whole family was on board, even Emma's boyfriend so yet another classic boating mistake, within two sentences. After the event I was counselled by many, far wiser, of the wisdom of committing one's inevitable first blunders alone, ensuring the family is not frightened to death, never to set foot on the boat again.

Of course you can't push start a boat! We needed to find a source of power to turn the engines over and on investigation were fortunate (or were we?) to find a haulage company, not far from the river, who loaned us a fully charged heavy-duty battery. This did the trick but in the excitement of the moment I failed to realise our window of opportunity for coping with the tides had passed.

Triumphantly we set off down the river from Torksey, heading into the characterless flat landscape where Nottinghamshire slips into Lincolnshire. We had no problem passing through the derelict delights offered by river-side Gainsborough. On, into a landscape getting ever bleaker and a depth getting ever more unpredictable. Ten miles before reaching the Humber we reached the river port of Keadby. Quite large ships make it up to here and I now realise the shrill burst of a ship's whistle, as we passed, was not a friendly greeting but a warning of impending doom. Oh I was so green!

Burton Staither comes next. How this part of England deserves a name is a mystery, there's nothing there except bleakness but it was at this spot the river took revenge on my ignorance. *The tide went out!* One moment we were afloat and the next, heeled over in nothing but sand. Upstream, beyond Newark, we had left a river wide and deep, pouring impressively over a number of weirs. How, at Burton Staither, does it just empty, to the extent you can get off and walk around the boat? This is exactly what our children did on that fateful day, whilst their mother was having her first boat related nervous breakdown. I promptly made a cup of tea, at forty-five degrees, but it didn't seem to help. Yes, the tide goes out but what happens to all of that water coming down at a good two knots at least?

No damage was sustained, except for a severely dented ego and after a wait sure enough the flood rushed back up the sandy riverbed to set us afloat again. By now our delayed entry into the Humber meant darkness had fallen giving us no choice but to pull ourselves together and navigate to Hull, which it has to be said we did with great success. We even felt quite proud of ourselves when finally we moored in the marina but it was the only time I have ever seen Janet take a nip of whisky. Needless to say we slept well, despite the marina being surrounded by the rather vibrant nightlife of Hull.

Unlike that very first attempt I now felt confident in my understanding of the river and it's perils. We departed Torksey at the optimum time and made our way with the ebbing tide, free of drama. After a few minutes jilling around just before Keadby, which is as far as we could go at low water, the flood of the new tide arrived on cue giving us more than adequate depth to progress through Burton Staither and enter the stark yet impressive bleakness of the Humber estuary. This vast expanse of brown turbulent water is not to be toyed with. It is the stuff of legend and anecdote among boaters from the Trent and the Ouse, the two constituent parts that feed this mighty stretch of water, draining a fifth of the country and creating the busiest shipping highway in Britain.

For those who are minded to face the challenge of the Humber there are rewards in plenty for a successful navigation into the estuary. Cruising under the vast span of the Humber Bridge, one of the longest suspension bridges in Europe, is an awe-inspiring experience, particularly after dark. Then, entering the haven of Hull Marina is both a comfort and a treat. But the greatest prize, after the boat is secured, harbour dues are settled and a steaming shower enjoyed, has to be pie, chips and a pint, at the riverside traditional hostelry, The Minerva!

4

...the hundred and something miles of North Sea

Without pressure on time we could luxuriate in allowing Hull to delay us for a couple of days. We always enjoyed a stay in the marina, either on our outward or inward journey but at the very least one night is essential to cope with tides and the sheer distance between available sanctuaries; that's unless you have a very fast vessel. The marina is a splendid transformation of a historic commercial dock, full of character and interest and offering a first chance to mix with yachts and other sea going types after the constraints of the river. It is also splendidly situated for the town centre, just a short walk away and it is this contrast that never fails to intrigue me; at one moment coping with the not insubstantial demands of the estuary and the next you are in the middle of things, mingling with throngs of shoppers going about a daily routine in this metropolitan normality.

This was even more acute when we sailed over to Holland on our first major sea crossing.

Summer holidays, August 1998. We planned to sail out of Lowestoft, for being the most easterly port in Britain it provides the ideal departure point to cross the North Sea or to arrive in the UK after a crossing. We had often watched the Dutch yachts arrive in Lowestoft; for many their idea of a weekend's entertainment was to race across the ocean. The most direct route leads to the Dutch port of Ijmuiden and this was to be our most ambitious voyage yet, a sea crossing which for some hours and for the first time would take us out of sight of land. Needless to say we were both excited and not a little apprehensive.

Waking up just after dawn to the most dreadful and depressing wail of a foghorn out on the sandbanks didn't help calm our anxiety and we concluded our departure was certain to be a non-starter. Disconcertingly the wail suddenly stopped and a brisk walk to look out over the harbour wall convinced us the early morning fog was burning off. With a rising sun our departure seemed to be possible after all. We knew the most difficult spot of navigation, when cruising from Lowestoft to the Dutch coast, is the immediate escape from Lowestoft; avoiding the notorious Holme Sand. It's crucial to pick up the South Holme cardinal buoy and, being a south cardinal, make sure our course is south of the treacherous sand banks. We were fortunate to follow out of the harbour an experienced Dutch couple on their yacht, also heading across to Ijmuiden, which helped give us confidence in our navigation. Once past the sand banks it's plain sailing with no further obstacles, apart from a hundred and something miles of North Sea!

It was the most amazing cruise, in brilliant sunshine and flat calm conditions. Our initial anxieties melted away and for most of the trip we could leave it to the autopilot, although I hasten to add, being alert sailors we always kept a good lookout and plotted our position hourly on the chart. A course of ninety degrees, or due east, for thirteen hours, delivered us to Ijmuiden harbour entrance and conveniently the south-north, flood-ebb, tidal flow looked after itself, six hours one way followed by six hours the other and we were back on the same course. The only time a course change became necessary was to avoid a… minor obstacle. We thought it prudent as we were heading for the impressive and definitely immovable structure of an oil-drilling platform, lurking just off the Dutch coast. Although not appearing on our chart its presence loomed up on our radar and heartened my reasoning to use the technology, even if the skies were perfectly clear.

We berthed in Ijmuiden feeling rather pleased with ourselves and a little bemused, even disappointed with the lack of any formality. No passport checks, no custom officer visits, in fact, no one knew we were there. Well, no doubt except for Dutch big brother. The authorities certainly didn't challenge us during our subsequent four-week trip that took us up the North Sea Canal, into Amsterdam and into the Ijsselmeer, the great inland sea.

Our return leg, back to British shores, was a little more eventful. We had made our leisurely way back to Seaport Marina on the coast at Ijmuiden but then six consecutively dreadful stormy days imprisoned us in port, along with a number of other stranded British boats. Before we could even contemplate the dash back across the North Sea conditions would have to calm down considerably and in the meantime we remained stranded in this convenient but rather expensive sanctuary.

It became apparent that certain developments were taking place shore-side and our investigations revealed we were in the centre of lavish preparation for the imminent Amsterdam Boat Show. It entertained us for a while, as we waited for that elusive weather window but wore thin when, on one of our daily visits to the marina office to pay yet another night's extortionate mooring, we were curtly asked to leave. Words to the effect, 'you will leave now', succinct and unequivocal. It seemed we were in the way; perhaps lowering the tone of the place as a flotilla of very impressive super yachts and exotic gin palaces was forming. As politely as I could, I enquired of the young lady whether she had taken a look over the harbour wall recently …or even been outside for the past week! Needless to say we were not to be ejected until the weather improved considerably.

When finally it felt safe to leave, the return voyage was far removed from the 'cruise' we enjoyed four weeks earlier. Sea conditions were marginal, certainly exciting and approaching the Suffolk coast, not only had darkness fallen but our tentative navigation back into Lowestoft was to be further complicated by pouring rain. After a crossing lasting twelve uncomfortable hours it required a supreme effort from both of us to concentrate on the buoyage leading safely back into port. This was apart from having to cope with a number of ships making their way down the coast. Janet has this nasty habit of hanging out of the saloon door, over the rail, binoculars slung round her neck, in the quest to spot a distant buoy. Each buoy has a unique pattern of flashing lights that have to be identified. Not only how many flashes but how many groups of flashes and what kind of flashes and what kinds of groups of flashes… Matching this information with that given on the charts is crucial when finding your way in an otherwise landmark-less seascape and in the treacherous seas around the east coast there is little room for error. Imagine the scene. I have one hand on the helm, struggling to keep 'Starry Vere' on course and the other on the tail of Janet's coat as she leans out over the sea but she is certainly very adept at night-time buoy spotting.

We berthed in the basin belonging to the Royal Norfolk and Suffolk Yacht Club, this at the time being the only place to berth in Lowestoft harbour and quite exhausted collapsed into a welcome bunk. Our plan was to wake promptly and make an early start on the twelve-hour passage up the coast to Grimsby. We needed to get back as the time to return to the world of work was drawing near.

A couple of fruity boat engines woke me from a deep sleep. It was still dark but peering out of the window into the gloom I could make out the good ship *Seletar* departing. Both boat and owners, Des and Shirley, two ancient mariners, who also hail from Farndon, were familiar to us. (I'm sure I'll be forgiven for the ancient) By the time I'd clambered out of bed and dutifully put the kettle to work, the sound of engines signalled *Seletar's* unexpected return. Odd, we thought and anxious to ensure that all was well with both boat and crew I popped round to say hello. All was well on board but the problem was the sea state. It transpired it was rather rough despite, or in spite of, an ok shipping forecast. Des and Shirley had thought better of it and as they have far more experience than us, we decided to take their lead and spend a day in Lowestoft.

That day turned into five, before the weather eased sufficiently to allow *Starry Vere* and *Seletar* to make an uncomfortable trip up the coast in convoy. By now it was early September so our approach to the Humber came in darkness once more. It was just after high water, there were ships everywhere and with only a one and a half-hour window each side of high water in which to lock through into the old fish dock, we had to find Grimsby! We were late but Shirley called up the lock keeper on the VHF radio and melted his heart; if we put a spurt on we'd be allowed through. Even with the wonders of GPS Grimsby harbour is not easy to find when the Humber ebb is determined to whisk you back out into the open sea, but we made it. The lock keeper insisted on squeezing both boats into the lock together, to this day I'm not sure how it was possible and we entered a tranquil, if slightly smelly, fish dock.

Wearily but with relief we made our way through the old port, past the remnants of a once enormous and proud fishing fleet, to the pleasure craft moorings run by the Humber Cruising Association. In a rather surreal situation we were welcomed by an excited group of folk more interested in selling us tickets for a barbecue than helping us find a spot for the night. It transpired we had arrived on the night of the association's end of season bash, which was in full swing. *"No! Sorry!"* We were not in the mood for socialising, preferring to enjoy a bite to eat and a tot of whisky on board *Seletar*. There was one last bizarre twist before the day was out. Half way through our pizza Janet and I remembered that, that very night, Ben was on the TV. He was performing with the European Union Youth Orchestra in a Prom concert, live from London's Royal Albert Hall. A portable TV was quickly produced and sure enough the concert was in full flight, an exhilarating performance of the epic Alpine Symphony by Richard Strauss. We spotted Ben playing among the first violins and rejoiced in the strangeness of life, well certainly of *our* lives. For when we were battling with the elements entering the Humber, Ben was blissfully unaware, putting on his black tie for the sophistication of a London concert.

Exhausted, yet happy, we retired to our bunks. I'm told there was a disco in the building virtually next to *Starry Vere*. I didn't hear a thing!

5

.....*the East Docking buoy*

Although we now had plenty of time to linger on this our final stay in Hull, we did have to keep an eye on the weather. The East Coast is notorious for its lack of harbours; once the Humber has been negotiated there's not a suitable refuge until reaching the East Anglian ports of Great Yarmouth and Lowestoft, unless you have some very local specialised knowledge. Grimsby, situated at the mouth of the estuary, would have normally been our next port of call and the long cruise down the coast is probably best started from here. But, as always, we are at the behest of tides as well as weather and these can create problems getting out of Grimsby in order to maximise daytime sailing. On this our farewell trip down the Humber, we were fortunate; a convenient high-water time presented us with the option of departing Hull at dawn and making the trip down to Lowestoft in one hop. Thirteen hours plus but the long days of June meant it would all be done in daylight.

The log entry gives 0555 as our time of departure from Hull. How I could be so precise at that time of the morning beats me but it was certainly gloomy as we left the shelter of the marina, passing through the sea lock and entering the estuary, just on high water. The shipping forecast was fine but the day had dawned damp and overcast and as we headed downstream my thoughts dwelt on the warm bed recently vacated. The immediate challenges soon focused the mind though, with high water the cue for ships of all shapes and sizes to start making passage down the estuary, utilising the rapidly increasing flow of the ebb. Buoys to be spotted, ships to be watched, this great highway is a challenge for the couple of hours it takes to reach its mouth, passing Spurn Point on our port side and Bull Sand Fort on our starboard.

Once past the Bull anchorage we could relax a little. The trip from Hull down to Lowestoft is a long one, some one hundred and twenty nautical miles and it can become tedious. As we passed down the Lincolnshire coast, a safe distance off the notorious Hail Sand, we settled into a routine of spotting the buoyage of our chosen route. *Rosse Spit, Protector, Inner Dowsing, North Docking*, the very names of these buoys immediately evokes a grey empty sea. First a dot in the distance, perhaps two or three miles away. As the distance closes, we make out its red comforting shape. Triumphantly we spot its name and watch it slowly pass into our wake. Then, binoculars raised, we repeat the process and scan the horizon for the next dot. Of course with the wonder of GPS the distance to each buoy and the course to steer is constantly available, once the desired latitude and longitude waypoints have been entered into the technology. But quite simply, the hunt for buoys gives us something to do and encourages us to keep the good lookout required by the International Regulations for the Prevention of Collision at Sea, the rules of the road!

Janet never suffers from seasickness. She has never quite managed to swim and if the shower is too fierce or the bath water above an inch deep panic can set in. Yet in a boat, be it negotiating locks on the canals or cruising out at sea, she is like an old hand. Sorry, perhaps *experienced* hand would be better? It is the same gritty determination you need to be a professional musician, particularly playing the oboe.

Unfortunately, on occasion, I do feel a little queasy. I've never been able to pinpoint why or when. On some trips the sea can be quite rough and I don't have a problem. Then there are other times when the going is calm and I begin to feel a little green. This trip proved to be one of those days and although the sea state seemed fine, I wasn't. It was most frustrating. Here we were, embarking on a new life, when this would be the norm. Was I doing the right thing? I suspect it was a combination of an insistent swell which, while not feeling uncomfortable, did consist of long nauseating rolls, coupled with the heady senses of excitement and apprehension. In the end I had to entrust the boat to Janet's care and simply lie down for a couple of hours.

The coast gradually recedes as we move out into the wide-open shallow waters of The Wash. Finally we lose sight of land completely until the pencil line of the flat north Norfolk coast reluctantly emerges over our starboard bow, usually when we are in the vicinity of the East Docking buoy. *The East Docking buoy*, now there's a name to conjure with, if you are a member of the Nabarro family, for it was at this very spot we reached the climax, the grand finale of that first summer holiday cruise. No, I'm ashamed to say the episodes of the flat batteries and grounding in the Trent were not the worst of it...

*

It was not long before we felt refreshed enough from our encounter with the bottom at Burton Staither to begin enjoying the sights and sounds of Hull. The sounds in particular were much to our delight; we had arrived in the middle of a Jazz festival taking place in the Marina. The weather was fine and sunny and the carnival atmosphere soon persuaded us that boating was fun after all. In fact we were so seduced that plans to resume our cruise down the coast were resurrected, with all hands keen to continue. Now, although it may seem I was unprepared, I had indeed laboured over this passage to the best that my one-year of night school allowed. What I hadn't grasped was the scale of the distance and for some unknown reason, the simple equation that one hundred and twenty nautical miles could take fifteen hours to complete. Sheer inexperience meant that I had still not absorbed the concept of distance versus time; I was still in a road-travel mindset.

Innocently we departed Hull and cruised downstream in good weather, indeed in my favour the weather and shipping forecasts had all been checked and no problems were reported imminent. The notion of breaking the journey at Grimsby didn't enter my head - a big mistake - and we sailed happily out of the Humber and down the coast. All was fine, everyone on board contentedly enjoying the cruise, the new experience and even the sun. The buoys, now familiar but then novel, came and went, albeit slowly but tolerably in these favourable conditions. But gradually, very gradually, the sea state changed. The wind started to blow, a persistent nasty chop set in and we began to realise life was becoming a little more uncomfortable and even unpleasant. The time between each buoy now seemed interminable and as I poured over the charts (looking for a short cut perhaps?) the burden of skipper, as well as head of the family, weighed heavily on my shoulders. Although I had calculated tides and distances the part of the equation missing from my comprehension was simply our lack of speed. Perhaps I was over cautious with the engines. Certainly on the delivery trip the previous January we had not reached the potential cruising speed and maybe I was still conscious of this. If I had maintained a speed of eight knots my tidal calculations would have held good, progress would have been quicker and less impeded by the changing weather, plus, there wouldn't have been the unfolding drama to relate! I was to learn later we were suffering a classic case of wind over tide; the wind blowing in the opposite direction to the running tide and when compounded by the shallow sea found in this part of the world, the result is the particularly uncomfortable condition we were experiencing. Not necessarily dangerous but of course I didn't know that at the time. It just felt exhausting.

The situation deteriorated as one by one the crew began to wilt. Emma's boyfriend at the time was the first to succumb to seasickness, so consequently Emma was relieved of all other duties to mop his brow. Ben still felt able to take a turn on the helm but Janet began to prepare for the worst. In reality we were perfectly safe, the boat was stronger than all of us and in later more enlightened times we had persisted through similar weather and similar sea states without a worry. This time we were far from enlightened and becoming very worried.

As we approached yet another large red buoy, after what seemed an eternity steaming toward it, even Ben threw in the towel and launching himself prostrate onto the saloon seating let out his now endearing comment, *"well, it's all over then!"*

That left just me, hanging on to the helm and wondering what to do for the best. Lowestoft was still a very long way off. We had departed Hull at eight in the morning and it was now approaching six in the evening. Our speed had been incredibly slow. I took to circling the buoy, the East Docking buoy, hanging onto the comfort of its presence whilst deciding the best course of action. Eventually pride had to be swallowed and I put out a call on the VHF radio channel 16, the normal 'listening' channel.

'Yarmouth coastguard, Yarmouth coastguard; Starry Vere, Starry Vere'.

......**'Starry Vere this is Yarmouth Coastguard'.**

So immediate I nearly fell off the helm seat in shock! Were they sitting there waiting for it? After appraising them of our situation and position - trying to sound relaxed and cool, after all my request was simply for advice - their response was instant and unequivocal, the lifeboat was to be despatched. I had no further say in it. Well, my feelings ranged from grateful relief to serious embarrassment.

I hadn't noted that the infamous East Docking buoy is situated directly due north of the small Norfolk port of Wells next the Sea and it was to be the Wells lifeboat coming to our rescue. Before long the lifeboat coxswain made radio contact with instructions to progress on a course due south, toward the coast. It's amazing, with the sure knowledge that the cavalry was on its way, sea sickness abated, nervous breakdowns were put on hold and even the sea state seemed to improve. We all began to feel quite perky again, it was becoming a bit of an adventure.

The bright orange lifeboat was soon visible ploughing through the grey waves toward us. Drawing near it was skilfully manoeuvred alongside and a crewmember put aboard *Starry Vere* to offer comfort. He would also act as our pilot, for the plan was to eventually lead us into the somewhat tortuous entry of Wells harbour. The difficulty of a small tidal window and crossing the notorious sand bar to enter the poorly buoyed and shifting channel, leading up to Wells harbour wall, is well documented in the pilot guides and almanacs and had seemed to me not an option. I was probably correct in that assumption but now we had a boat-load of local knowledge to assist.

Lifeboat and *Starry Vere* had to wait off the coast for the tide to turn. The kettle was boiled, sandwiches made and our friendly lifeboat man turned out to be quite a character; it was very easy to forget why he was there. When the tide eventually permitted our entry dusk was falling and we were faced with the bizarre experience of being escorted into Wells, straight into the glare of numerous fish and chip shops, pubs and entertainment arcades, lining the harbour. We also found ourselves subject to the gaze of hoards of curious holidaymakers, keen to see the reason for the lifeboat's very public call out. No sooner had we moored safely then younger crewmembers, now fully recovered, made-off into the bright lights of Wells. Janet and I heaped copious and humble thanks on the lifeboat crew and then surrendered to the smell of fish and chips.
But still the humiliation wasn't over!

The following morning we were greeted by a stream of sightseers, anxious to inspect the casualty. An official from the Royal National Lifeboat Institute came aboard and very sensitively quizzed us about our experience. There was no hint of criticism, far from it and we were comforted by the fact that under the circumstances and in his opinion, we had done the right thing. It was some comfort but I still felt somewhat inadequate. But then we were taken aback when one of Janet's older oboe pupils from Nottingham appeared on the quayside. Janet was aware that this particular pupil, Zoë, 'did a bit of sailing', but what she was not fully aware of was the level of her expertise, which it transpires is very considerable. Also Zoë was accompanied by her parents, they were all on a family holiday in Wells, and Zoë's father is a Royal Yachting Association instructor. Of course we graciously welcomed them on board whilst wishing to descend from sight through a hole in the bottom of the boat. Our surprise was mutual as they were well aware of the Lifeboat's 'shout'; the volunteer crew is still summoned in the traditional way by firing a maroon into the air so the whole of Wells knew. Zoë's parents had a notion we were afloat but it was a surprise to find out who was the subject of the 'rescue'.

Over coffee the whole story unfolded. Zoë's father, an experienced mariner, and like the RNLI official, understanding and supportive, pointed out wisely that such misfortunes can catch anyone out at sea, it pays to be humble, an attitude which I have learnt to hold dear. The sea is always master.

We stayed put in Wells for over a week, enjoying the atmosphere of a small Norfolk town with a port sadly in decline but with still so much to offer. With the crew jumping ship to continue their summer holidays enjoying less dangerous pursuits, it was left to Janet and me to decide our next move. Despite earlier threats never to set foot on a boat again Janet did stay with it, much to her credit. We thought better of chancing our arm any further down the coast and having experienced more than enough excitement for one summer holiday decided to make the return trip back up to the Trent. Zoë made a lovely gesture by offering to crew with us back to Hull, with her father's blessing no less, which was very supportive. Having an experienced sailor on board made all the difference to our confidence and helped ensure a trouble free return trip. We made it back to Lincoln far wiser sailors than when we had left; that must be positive.

6

....boats is bovver!

As has become our tradition we drank a toast to the East Docking buoy while cruising past at a steady eight knots, heading for our rendezvous with the Norfolk coast. We had certainly gained a great deal of knowledge and experience since that fateful first voyage but passing the buoy remains a thoughtful and sobering moment, so sobering the toast was made with a mug of tea!

Our course took us to within sight of Cromer, where a couple of miles of attractive cliffs briefly present a more dramatic coastline. But our eyes remained vigilantly seaward, for this is the dreaded crab pot territory. Just a small white or red blob of a float on the surface is all you will see to mark the menace below, a potentially incapacitating line down to the pot on the seabed and a wide berth is essential because very rarely does the line sink vertically. Forces of wind and tide can set it at a deceptive angle and once snagged around propeller or rudder it's either a swim with a sharp knife, or a call for help. I didn't want to re-acquaint myself with the men and women of the Wells lifeboat, no matter how high I held them in my esteem and I certainly didn't fancy a swim.

Crab pots safely negotiated, we closed to within a mile of the coast at Winterton Ness and passed the wonderfully named Cockle Buoy with its ever-ringing bell. Here starts the last leg of the trip lying on a course due south, all the way down the East Anglian coast to Lowestoft. On the nautical charts the three main navigation channels are aptly named 'roads' and it is wise, nay essential, to stick rigidly to the white line! *Caister Road, Yarmouth Road* and *Corton Road* are buoyed channels offering a safe route down this treacherous portion of coastline where shoals or sandbanks lie very close in. It was here we came closer to the coastline beaches than at any other point on the trip and as we were nearing the tidal state of low water it was the seaward side presenting the greater danger. We could clearly see the waves breaking on the exposed sand of South Scroby but the route is well buoyed and offered no real threat as long as we held the correct course. We gave Great Yarmouth a miss and cruised on further to reach the distinctive rocket-like light towers that mark the welcoming and easy entrance into the port of Lowestoft. 1930 was logged as our time of arrival, a long day, longer than it had taken us to sail over to Holland in fact but seasickness aside it had been a rewarding cruise and satisfying to arrive without a hitch. With permission granted from the harbour master we made our way into the port, into the hallowed waters of the yacht basin and into a hot shower.

Lowestoft is a major port and the only one on the East Anglian coastline to offer access to any vessel at any state of the tide. Facilities for yachts and other pleasure craft are currently limited to those provided in the yacht basin by the Royal Norfolk and Suffolk Yacht Club, *"an amazing establishment"*, as Derek Bowskill describes it in his book, *The East Coast.*

"...in spite of being a relic, redolent of those dear, dead Edwardian days well beyond recall, it is alert and alive with the kind of humming activity that is not usually associated with yacht clubs. Stringent regulations control your sartorial style in various rooms, and while they don't actually have a string quartet for your leisure and pleasure at afternoon tea, they should, for it would complete the mise en scène".

I love Derek's wit and observation. In my opinion his writing is of a quality rare in nautical journalism and demonstrates the art of imparting information whilst still having a mind to literary quality. We were fortunate that Derek moored his boat *Valcon* at Farndon for much of the time we were there. He and I chatted a great deal and being well versed in the arts our meetings in adjacent showers always led to interesting discussions, refreshingly not always about boats. The one boaty thing I do remember well though was his wise quip, *"boats is bovver!"* On our journey down through the French canals another of his books, *From the Channel to the Med,* was our bible. We often chuckled when comparing his writing with the reality and hope our paths will cross again sometime so we can inform him of our enjoyment; over a glass of wine perhaps?

Derek will find many changes when next he sails into Lowestoft. The club still stands proudly and now safely, behind new security fencing. It remains an aristocratic beacon, seemingly oblivious to the plethora of tacky amusement arcades and fast food outlets that dare to overlook the south basin. The RN&SYC has made good use of EU monies; the basin bristles with state of the art pontoons and facilities in the majestic clubhouse are now unrecognisable from our earlier visits. All very well, but with a mooring charge identical to that which we later paid in both Paris and Barcelona and when extra is expected for water and electricity, then it's no wonder the many visiting yachtsmen, including many cruising over from Holland, consider the UK very expensive. I have recently heard that a civic run marina is to be fashioned from the old redundant Trawl Dock. Excellent! Healthy competition is just what's needed.

Budgetary constraints certainly wouldn't allow an extended stay in Lowestoft but our intention was to spend some time on the Norfolk Broads, a cruising ground we had yet to experience and as July was upon us we hoped for a pleasant spell of weather. Once through the efficient lifting road bridge and into the inner harbour, evocatively named Lake Lothing, Lowestoft provides the best access to the Broads. Best certainly but not straightforward, as the legendary Mutford Lock stands as an obstacle to be negotiated. When I called the port authority on the VHF radio to book passage through the road bridge, at one of the regular opening times, the lady on duty was immensely helpful and offered to inform the 'keeper of Mutford' of our wish to use the lock the following morning. Phew! I was glad she spoke to him and not me. The lock, built over 150 years ago with the unusual feature of gates that face both ways, was designed to offer speedy access to the Broads at any state of the tide. The reality, in our experience, has been access only at the behest and goodwill of the relevant authority, whose policy is enthusiastically enforced by a keeper intent on extracting every bit of gratitude from his 'customers'. What's more, adding insult to injury, an extortionate charge is levied for this service. We mustn't complain too much as there was a time not so long past when the lock only opened once a week. It's hard to comprehend how such policies are tolerated in an area with such a reliance on tourism.

Maximising our short stay in the regal Yacht basin we delayed passing through the road bridge into Lake Lothing until late afternoon. All kind of marine refurbishment takes place in this stretch of water, with large commercial quays and yards at the seaward end and an abundance of small craft in every state of repair and dilapidation further in. We lowered our radar mast, enabling us to creep under the first hurdle of the ancient railway swing-bridge and moored on the waiting pontoon just before the lock. The pontoon is marooned in the middle of nowhere, an island without access to the shore. Someone has decided it is certainly not to be anything other than a waiting pontoon but that suited us; we were secure for the night and poised to do battle first thing in the morning.

Nine o'clock sharp the 'keeper of Mutford', all of fifty yards away and clearly visible in his watchtower, called on the VHF to grant us permission to lock through. At least when it happened it was quick and efficient and after handing over six pounds for the privilege we were able to enter the vastly different world of Oulton Broad, the gateway to the southern Broads. It's only a short hop from the lock to the grandly named Oulton Yacht Station and here we moored among the motor cruisers with not a yacht in sight.

The impressive Oulton Broad is probably the best known and one of the largest expanses of water in the Broads system. With around one hundred and thirty acres of navigable water, its immense popularity as a water-sport recreation area can create tricky conditions for navigating.

Craft of all shapes, sizes, power source and crew competence, dodge around in every direction and at all speeds but the yacht station is a lovely place to just sit and watch this variety of marine activity sail by. In season it's a popular watering hole for the many hire boats and as they are requested by the efficient staff to moor 'stern to', perhaps *ordered* would be a more appropriate description, a degree of entertainment is often forthcoming. Oddly, whilst moored at the Yacht Station, it is not necessary to purchase a Broads Authority licence but as soon as you untie those mooring ropes liability becomes due. We purchased a permit covering a couple of weeks and set off to explore these famous waterways that started life as peat diggings!

7

.....still attired in night wear

Oulton Broad is connected to the rest of the Broads by the short stretch of waterway known as Oulton Dyke and cruising this watery link we were transported from the almost suburban environs of Oulton, constantly alive and busy, into an atmosphere of rural tranquillity, a characteristic Broads world of marshland, edged by mile after mile of tall dense reed beds. The Dyke leads to the first major river of the Broads, the Waveney, and to the simple choice of turning either to port or starboard; the former leading up to Beccles and the latter to the rest of the Broads network. We had time to explore so it was a turn to port and a gentle cruise up the river.

The Waveney River Centre looked attractive enough as we passed it on our starboard side and with its good size mooring basin and abundance of facilities it was obviously being enjoyed by a large number of holidaymaking boaters. We rather fancied a quiet secluded spot for the night, in this beautiful remote area but it soon became clear an impromptu bank-side mooring might be a problem. The reed beds are incessant and impenetrable, preventing any contact with dry land and importantly, finding something suitably permanent to tie to. The Broads Authority have constructed a number of two or three-boat mooring areas but we were finding these already occupied and it was beginning to look as if it would have to be back to the River Centre. I had though noticed an old tree stump protruding through the reeds, right on the edge of the river and maybe with the potential to at least give us a secure mooring for a night. We circled round cautiously, checking for any other remaining parts of the long-dead tree that might be lurking below the surface. The depth seemed ok so we edged up close, gently bringing *Starry Vere's* bow toward the stump where Janet, with her growing rope handling skill that was to peak on the canals of France, adroitly lassoed it. The river was on the ebb with a modest current helpfully drawing us back snugly into the reeds. There was certainly no way on or off the boat but, as evening began to draw in, dinner was quickly under way and with a cork to pull we felt quite comfortable. I hadn't forgotten about the tide and decided to throw out a kedge anchor from the stern, thinking this would be enough to hold *Starry Vere* in place when the inward flood began its return; due sometime in the middle of the night.

It was pitch black when, waking with a start, I instinctively knew something was untoward. The feel of the boat, an unusual sound, you soon become very sensitive to the smallest change from the norm. The night was very, very dark but as I pulled a curtain aside our little problem became immediately obvious. I should have been peering into the bank-side reed bed but even with limited visibility it was plain to see I was looking straight down the course of the river. We had swung out at ninety degrees to the bank and the bow rope around the tree trunk was straining and creaking under the tension of the incoming flood.

In the blackness we reluctantly clambered out of a warm bed, resisting the instinct to turn on the interior lights as this would have put paid to our night vision and grabbing a torch, headed out on deck to be met by drizzle and gloom. The strain on the rope had pulled the bow up tight to the tree trunk and I was worried something would give; we needed to release the pressure on the rope and worry about an alternate mooring later. So first to the stern, to ascertain the whereabouts of the kedge anchor. It had spectacularly failed to do its job and I just hoped the rope had not snagged around prop or rudder. Thankfully I was able to pull it onboard without a problem, except for oodles of thick Broads mud. Back to the bow and it seemed the only way to slacken the rope, other than taking a knife to it, would be to start the engines and run the boat forward into the reeds, far enough for Janet to be able to lean over the front of the boat, the pulpit is the nautical term, and release her lasso. The sound of engines firing up intruded horribly into a very still night and tentatively I engaged slow ahead. The bow pushed into the reeds illuminated solely by our steaming light on the front mast... and then, despite the chill and the uncertainty of our situation... a smile must have crossed my face. I certainly wouldn't wish to compromise Janet's dignity... but... as she leaned over the pulpit... grappling with the rope... and... still attired in nightwear... short summer nightwear... well... I can say no more, except... she did a splendid job freeing the rope. Regaining my composure I reversed the boat slowly back from the bank and contemplated our situation as we wallowed in the middle of the river.

Beyond the illuminated foredeck visibility was just about zero, particularly as the heavy drizzle was now playing havoc with my specs, or had they just steamed up? There was no way we could resume our mooring at this spot and it seemed the only choice was to carefully proceed back down the river and find a mooring at the River Centre. Dead slow we edged forward and Janet took up what we now know as the 'Titanic' position, right on the bow. Still attired in her M&S special she horizontally thrust out either right or left arm, depending on which way I needed to steer to keep in the middle of the river. Perhaps Worzel Gummage would have been a better description than Kate Winslett but this unorthodox yet effective method of communication kept us safely in the channel for what seemed an eternity until the River Centre appeared out of the gloom. A small security light had been left on to weakly illuminate a fuel dock but drawing alongside a moan of desperation came out of the blackness. Janet, poised with mooring rope, realised the high tide had raised the water level up to the height of the bank, which from *Starry Vere's* already relatively high gunnel meant a substantial leap onto a bank-side she actually couldn't see! But leap she did and although it was not to be witnessed her landing was evidently completed with an Olympic standard double role. Finally, safe and secure, we took stock. It was after two o'clock but the excitement had left us wide-awake. There was only one thing for it, a mug of steaming cocoa and a piece of sustaining ship's fruit cake.

The following day dawned with the damp greyness persisting; in fact it persisted for most of our time on the Broads, demanding very unseasonable hot water bottles and warm clothing. We decided not to give up on the river and continued our exploration back upstream, giving the infamous tree trunk a wide berth and this time managed to secure to a mooring at one of the few bank-side spots available and within walking distance of Beccles. Realising our parking place here in July was about as sought after as a car parking spot in a Saturday afternoon high street shopping area, we set out on foot to explore this charming small Suffolk town which anyway is the head of the navigation and now a very popular and characterful tourist spot.

Our return trip down the river for the second time was made more comfortably in broad daylight. Past the junction with Oulton Dyke and on down the undemanding reed-lined channel to the first of a number of steel-girdered railway swing bridges, found on the Broads. The pilot book advises, on approach, to give three blasts on the ships whistle to attract the keeper's attention. We were set to relish this moment, for *Starry Vere* is equipped with a couple of impressive air horns and very rarely do we get the chance to sound them. We approached the bridge, Janet, as the owner of the lucky digit assigned the task, poised over the button and then, push! Something like one second of wheeze is all we got, followed by a deafening silence. To add insult to injury the bridge gently swung open anyway; for it appears despite the instruction in the pilot book the keepers are so attentive it is never necessary to abuse the Broads tranquillity. Investigating our humiliating failure later, I had put a fuse in the horn circuit too small for the job.

We lingered for a couple of days at the riverside village of Reedham and although a very popular spot, with its grassy bank-side moorings packed with hire boating holidaymakers - this was supposed to be high summer after all - it manages to remain an unspoilt and attractive Broads community. We had one or two close encounters with the hire boats, or 'bumper boats' as we came to call them in France but the weather was so miserable, so cold, we felt very sorry for the many families who had paid not inconsiderable sums to enjoy a couple of weeks boating in the sunshine.

Cruising on in the dampness we gave the blot on the landscape that is Cantley sugar beet factory and the Red House pub next door a miss and took a soggy mooring, just above a grand mansion of a pub called the Beauchamp Arms.

The rain was becoming incessant and as the river is still tidal we watched the level rise alarmingly, to the point of spilling over onto the bank-side path. With wellington boots dug out of winter storage, I jumped off the boat into an inch or so of water and attempted to adjust fenders that were beginning to float away from the side of the hull. We tried to eat dinner but with one eye, no all eyes, on the river, willing the tide to turn and in desperation we made a pact that dessert would not be served until the many pieces of driftwood were spotted returning back downstream. With our noses pushed to the damp glass, like a couple of children peering into a sweet shop, we watched and waited until the tide nonchalantly turned. With relief we celebrated with the rather special Chocolate-topped Sharp Lemon Cake, which Janet had created from the Josceline Dimbleby cookbook. Vacillation of weather rarely hampers *Starry Vere's* culinary delights.

We had a mind to reach the city of Norwich but en-route we first encountered the sophistication of Brundall, a Broads village *superieur*, with its wonderful array of individual waterside properties and the birthplace of the famous Broom family of motorboats. We moored at a lovely spot, just past the village, on the edge of a wood through which it was necessary to walk to get anywhere. It was interesting to see the Broom works and boatyard despite my cynicism at the gin-palace image. It's a famous name and each vessel seems to be individually constructed in the relatively modest Brundall yard. Probably great personal service, if you've got the cash.

For such a fine East Anglian city the approach to Norwich by river is very uninspiring, lined as it is with industrial units in various states of dereliction. The Carrow Road lifting bridge is well organised for boaters but the main impediment should have been the famous railway swing bridge. Our inward passage went with such ease we assumed its reputation for difficulty was no more than folklore. Trying to escape was to be a different story and all in all we wished we hadn't bothered with Norwich as securing a mooring also proved a problem. There is the 'Yacht Station', but this is only available by passing under a fixed road bridge far too low for *Starry Vere*. Immediately before the road bridge a large restaurant barge had taken up permanent residence and before that lay the only bit of quay that seemed suitable for us to make fast. But still not without problems, for adjacent to this part of the river a large development site was in the final stages of construction. One of those multi-purpose entertainment complexes, containing shops, cinemas, and clubs. Also, the whole quayside was posted with temporary 'No Mooring' signs. A small problem and not particularly welcoming but after making it this far we were determined to spend at least one night in the historic city. We concluded the discouragement to moor was probably a leftover from when the building site was at a more dangerous stage so we decided to chance it. Anyway, surely the rail bridge wouldn't open twice in one day!

The night was noisy and a little threatening but the only 'danger' was from the nightlife of Norwich and not anything structural. This new centre was obviously where it was at in the city and as so often happens, we were going to bed as large swathes of the population were just embarking on their evening entertainment. Consequently, come the morning, we were keen to be off but between us and tranquillity stood the imposing steel structure of the rail bridge.

I began calling the bridge operator on the VHF radio as we slipped our mooring but approaching the grey and now very permanent looking structure there still hadn't been a response. The bank-side approach to the bridge is not very inviting on either side, meaning an uncomfortable jilling around in the centre of the river while I continued to attempt radio contact. Still no response. This was more like it, more in keeping with the bridge's reputation. With frustration mounting I resorted to the mobile phone. Directory Enquiries gave me a number to try and to my utter amazement and pleasure I found myself talking to none less than Railtrack, head office, London! The lady I was speaking to was equally amazed, particularly when I informed her I was calling from a boat, stuck in the middle of a river, with the failure of the bridge operator to respond causing me a big problem. It certainly did the trick, butt was kicked as they say, for not many minutes later an anonymous operator pulled a switch and the bridge eased open.

We retraced our steps out of the city and enjoyed returning to Broads solitude, lingering at many of the moorings we had discovered a few days before. Cruising back through Reedham we took the left turn of the River Yare, which of course could take us to Yarmouth. It was not our intention to visit Great Yarmouth but memories come flooding back of one of the most 'memorable' concerts I have ever conducted and Janet has ever played in. Someone in the town's entertainment department, a deluded soul who probably lost their job, came up with the idea of promoting a Viennese concert... in the variety theatre... at the end of the pier... in February. Instruments, music, everything had to be wheeled down the length of a wintry, wind swept pier. Imagine the lovely moment when Brian, harpist with the orchestra, trundled his splendid golden harp down past the bingo players; a vision of heaven for some no doubt. But most of all, I will never forget the experience of conducting The Blue Danube Waltz, accompanied by the sound of the North Sea pounding beneath the stage and yes, with an audience consisting of the famous one man and his dog!!

The grey-green of Breydon Water was now our objective, similarly immortalised in words and music. Just before the river spills out into Breydon a delightful postcard scene of windmill and ancient pub presented itself. The hostelry, The Berney Arms, sports the distinction of being unique in the UK; allegedly access is only possible by water or on foot. Allegedly! The give-away scene of a Range Rover secreted behind the pub buildings sadly dispelled this romantic notion.

It's a four-mile cruise across the wonderfully desolate and evocative expanse of Breydon, with its population of black cormorants and shags so germane to the scene. The navigable channel is well marked by stakes and it is wise not to deviate for this is an inland-sea of mud, thinly disguised as water by no more than a shallow covering. The New Breydon Bridge provides the gateway into Yarmouth but we returned to the Berney Arms and spent a night on the wall next to the pub, happily exchanging the five-pound mooring fee for our entitlement of five pounds worth of beer.

The two-week permit to navigate was near to expiring but in any case we were more than ready to leave the July chill of the Broads and thought it easiest to return to the sea via Oulton, Mutford Lock and Lowestoft. Our next port of call was to be a sentimental journey up the River Orwell to Ipswich.

A day cruising took us back to the Yacht Station at Oulton and the following morning I walked round to the lock with the aim of negotiating a passage through, sometime during the day. The pile of industrial bits on the side of the lock didn't bode well and sure enough the antique machinery, that of the lock gates not the lock keeper, had recently just disintegrated. The dreary prognosis was of at least a couple of weeks before a repair might be complete. Why someone hadn't hit on the idea of posting this information at key spots throughout the Broads was a surprise. A bank-side notice or a sign on a few bridges could have saved us and no doubt others a couple of unnecessary day's cruising. There is only one other exit to the sea; it looked as though we were going to savour the delights of Great Yarmouth after all.

The unplanned second cruise through Breydon was a welcome bonus and the New Bridge didn't present a problem as its available height is more than sufficient for *Starry Vere*. But now, after a couple of weeks on inland waterways, we needed to get our brains in gear. Negotiating the busy road crossing, the Haven Bridge at

Yarmouth, is a precise operation and via the VHF radio the keeper gave us clear instructions on how he wished us to proceed. Thankfully the wait was short because the current through the harbour, be it flood or ebb, is stunning. I had only read about it and what I had read underplayed the reality!

The stream of vehicles on the busy main road through Great Yarmouth came to what I'm sure was a reluctant halt to allow the bridge to lift. We were chivvied through, along with a couple of Yachts and then mooring on the Town Hall quay, just below the bridge, was the next challenge. It's the only spot for us pleasure-boaters and we needed to stop and check that the weather was going to be kind for our eventual exit into the sea. Approaching and securing to the high wall, in one of the strongest currents I have ever experienced, was a test for us both. Even when secure we spent hours resetting and refining our ropes to accommodate the fantastic rise and fall of the tide, twice every twenty-four hours. Passing through Breydon had taken us in one swoop from a recreational world to another, serious and sea going.

The morning before we left Yarmouth we were treated to a bizarre experience both humorous and alarming. Janet and I were still in bed, enjoying that semi-conscious state. Yes, such was the time it should have been otherwise.

A distinctive engine sound passed by.

"The hire boats are making an early start", Janet mused.

"HIRE BOAT!"

It couldn't be, but pulling back the curtain...it certainly was. A Broads hire cruiser, draped with an extended family, chugging happily down the river and heading straight for the North Sea. By the time I had dragged on some clothes and climbed out onto the foredeck the hire boat had reached the large ships moored on each side of the harbour. Eventually someone on the hire boat must have realised that perhaps they were in an alien environment, or perhaps someone on a ship had 'gently' advised them. The boat, very delicately, made an about turn into the current and with clouds of smoke pouring from the exhaust of an engine just offered a challenge, it began a slow and laboured return back upstream whence it came. If the engine had failed or overheated, which it was quite entitled to do, the outcome may have been more serious than humorous but thankfully it didn't. They weren't the first and probably won't be the last. There's a lovely story told of a hire boat that made the same error, except they just kept going, out into the sea, a right turn down the coast, another right into Lowestoft harbour and back into the Broads. Unperturbed, so the story goes, the family on board thought the North Sea was just another large Broad!

8

...canned music, canned drink

Our exit from Yarmouth needed careful consideration. The quite astonishing speed of the tidal flow could make entering or leaving the port a little tricky if the rhythm of the tides and their effect on the whole of our coastline is not understood. On the eastern side of the country the tide *floods* (comes in) with a north to south flow, from the top of Scotland, right down the east coast, meeting the incoming west-east flood along the south coast in the Dover area. Conversely, the *ebb* (going out) retreats in the opposite direction and this sequence happens twice in a twenty-four hour period, day in and day out; certainly one of the certainties of life like day and night. We needed to leave our mooring on the River Yare to follow its flow out into the sea and take a right, continuing south down the coast toward Harwich. The current, up and down the river through Yarmouth, slackens twice each tide as it reaches high water and low. It's a remarkable phenomenon when the current simply stops, leaving a brief window where the river becomes a docile lake. This calm before the storm is the ideal time to leave but it then depends if your plan is to turn left, on a northerly course up the coast, or right, aiming south. Do we leave on high water or low? It's not rocket science but with this understanding life aboard can be far more pleasant and particularly rewarding as you work in partnership with the forces of nature. We wanted to cruise south, so it would be best to harness the southerly flood and I reckoned this meant leaving on low water. If my timing was correct we should have ample time to exit the river and re-enter the sea, just as the tide resumes its relentless drive south. With tide tables pronouncing low water on this day as six-thirty in the morning we had an early start. The weather seemed to be improving at last and with a beautiful July morning promising sunshine and light winds, the omens were good.

Sure enough the cruise down the Suffolk coast was just perfect and by lunch-time we were passing Harwich and entering the River Orwell, with still a couple of hours of flood to help us on our way. The good weather had also encouraged the large sailing fraternity of these parts out onto the river, keeping us watchful but adding to the pleasure of our stately procession up the ten miles to the port of Ipswich.

My memories of the couple of months spent in the town, during the period between purchasing the boat and eventually leaving, are of intense excitement. I was working part-time in Lincolnshire, a return to the teaching profession but at every opportunity I would drive down to Suffolk like a child at Christmas. It was a wonderful period of discovery as the new acquisition was explored from bow to stern with the opportunities racing through my mind.

It had been just under five years since the motley crew, me included as novice, had departed in 'Mailoma' and sailed her up the coast on the delivery trip to Lincoln. I had always been determined to return under my own command, as it were to come full circle, to mark a very personal achievement. I had acquired many skills, accumulated a modest knowledge of navigation and seafaring and the boat was obviously on its way to being well preserved. If the truth were known it might also mollify the doubters who saw no future in a landlubber buying and coping with such a vessel, a first boat as well. Strange effects these boats have on men!

One very welcome development since our protracted departure five years earlier, is the greatly improved twenty-four hour lock access in and out of the historic Ipswich dock. The River Orwell is navigable at all states of the tide but access to the dock was limited to a window an hour or so either side of high water. This presented a very limited opportunity to leave the dock, particularly if the intent was just to enjoy the river and then return and I'm sure Neptune Marine and the other marinas in the dock are now probably far more attractive propositions for the pleasure boater.

We made fast to the floating pontoons at Neptune in time for a late lunch. Our arrival had been greeted by a lovely moment when I spotted Alan, probably best described as marina foreman, although I suspect he has a greater involvement in the ownership of the place than originally imagined. He was busy working on a nearby boat when he glanced up, down and then the double take as he recognised the boat. Alan maintained 'Mailoma' for her previous owner and indeed had often taken her out on fishing trips. He'd been a font of information and I was particularly pleased to meet him again but I will dwell on my motives no further.

There was a secondary reason for spending a week in Ipswich. Stowed in my ten percent 'half' of the double wardrobe, and much to my chagrin, was a navy blue suit, white shirt, black shoes and even a tie! Janet's ninety percent 'half' was crammed with a choice of outfits… we were going to a wedding. In truth we were both looking forward to it very much as Ben was to be best man, his long-standing friends were the lucky bride and groom, plus a wonderful bonus, Emma had been invited to sing at the reception.

Emma and partner Adam hired a car and drove down to stay with us on the boat. The wedding was in nearby Cambridgeshire and come a fine and sunny Saturday morning we must have presented an unusual scene in the marina as we processed off the boat and along the pontoons, dressed in our finery. We crept back in the early hours and the blue suit has not seen the light of day since.

Emma and Adam left us for their drive back up to Leeds and with all ghosts now put to rest we made our own preparations to leave Ipswich, bound for the Thames Estuary. Our itinerary was beginning to look like a series of social engagements, for now we were on our way to a golden wedding anniversary party in Maidstone and conveniently for us Maidstone sits as far as we can navigate up the River Medway, reached from the mouth of the Thames.

Of the Thames estuary Derek Bowskill writes, *"it can furnish some of the nastiest waters in the world"*, a warning of such gravity that can't be ignored, especially when about to embark on the trip for the first time. So homework was undertaken with diligence. Charts studied, GPS armed, weather forecasts scrutinised, we were well prepared but the reality was an absolute dream. The mighty Thames was calm and very gentle, our luck was in and we had the opportunity to enjoy the classic passage and some historic landmarks.

To make best use of the flood tide I had calculated we should leave Ipswich at about 1230. Daylight availability shouldn't be a problem but when the morning is bright and calm it makes for a very itchy wait, I was keen to be off. Common sense prevailed and the log gives 1250 as our time of departure. Studying the estuary chart I was confronted by a number of route options. We chose the rather depressing sounding Black Deep channel.

After clearing Harwich and picking our way across the shallows of the Medussa Channel, off the Naze, it was heartening to spot a small coaster approaching on our port bow, seemingly set on the same course; we weren't alone. We tailed it for much of the afternoon but it had the edge on our eight knots and gradually pulled away. No matter, it was a wonderful cruise and we had splendid views of a number of wartime relics such as Knock John Tower and the amazing Shivering Sands Towers.

Most amazing of all though is the wreck of the *Richard Montgomery*, lying just outside the entrance to the River Medway. This United States Navy ship went down in the Second World War and portions of its ghostly superstructure, pushing up through the water, is sobering enough. What is awesome is this ship was fully loaded with ammunition when it went down and its deadly cargo is still on board. Opinion varies to the threat posed today but the wreck is well buoyed and naturally the subject of an exclusion zone. We were pleased to see this famous 'landmark' alongside the channel into the Medway and pleased to be passed it, particularly as the scene was made a little more threatening by the failing light.

We were aiming for Queensborough, just a little way into the Medway proper and then a turn to port into the River Swale, the river that makes the Isle of Sheppey an island. Our plan was to pick up a buoy off Queensborough for the night but easier said than done, first find a vacant buoy. We tentatively cruised up and down the lines of moored boats but certainly anything looking substantial enough to give us peace of mind overnight was already occupied. We made one attempt at a smaller pink specimen but our experience of picking up a buoy as the boat bobs about on a choppy sea was severely limited and, although Janet made a valiant effort, hanging over the bow with a boat hook, the growing gloom convinced me we needed to promptly seek out an alternative. In the centre of the river sit a row of very sad looking large vessels, ships indeed, which, either floating or sitting on the bottom, are peacefully rotting away. Moored to one of these relics was a tug, probably there for the night and we went alongside to ask if we could raft up. The response was cool, that was plain enough even though we couldn't begin to recognise the language. It was clear we were not welcome but a crewmember did gesture to the other side of the hulk. Fine, that will do, so we motored round and moored alongside a rusty heap that at one time would have been a ship. As an overnight stop it was excellent, not very scenic, but good enough.

Once again tides dictated our departure, we needed to make our way up the Medway on the flood and as the optimum time was first light we slipped away from our ghostly relic in the early morning greyness. We hadn't noticed, in our anxiety to find a mooring the previous night but leaving we spotted, among the row of rusting specimens, the 60's pirate radio ship *Radio Caroline*, still complete with transmitting masts and aerials.

Initially the Medway is still a major seaway with large ships coming and going. Up to Gillingham it is wide and wild with endless creeks, islands and mud flats. After Gillingham discipline sets in and as the banks draw in closer the channel begins to take on the more comfortable conventional form of a river. We were now into an extremely popular cruising ground as the well-buoyed channel picked its way between line upon line of yacht moorings. History, particularly that military, is also all around. Chatham's historic dockyard, now a museum, marina and fashionable place to live, can just be seen on the port side but we spotted a variety of smaller and obviously still active military bases. Two large sweeping bends and we were confronted by Rochester Bridge, fixed and therefore the limit of navigation for yachts. The pilot books for the Medway dwell on the potential problems of available depth in the vicinity of the bridge so as we passed under its steely span I was half expecting to touch bottom. We were aiming to make the passage on one tide, so we had to reach Rochester promptly to give us the flood up to Allington Lock and the end of the tidal section. Too early and we could find those shoal patches which are supposed to be a danger. But all was well, tidal calculations must have been fine and our passage up to Allington was made safely if not with scenic satisfaction. There are lovely moments such as the old arched bridge at Aylesford but generally the upper reaches of the tidal Medway are not attractive. We were horrified, on a couple of occasions, to see bright red effluent running into the river from the paper producing plants.

With some relief we locked through Allington and into a different world of beautiful riverside properties and overhanging trees forming a romantic canopy over the slow moving river. This delightful pastoral scene was not to last. A couple of gentle miles on and bang, we sailed unsuspectingly right into the middle of Maidstone's annual riverside festival. Boats bedecked with flags and streamers, canned music, canned drink, canned hot dogs, even canned people... we were to become reluctant exhibits for the throngs of folk strolling up and down the quay, enjoying a week of non-stop entertainment and riverside happenings.

The town had played an important part in my earlier life with most of my extended family hailing from Kent. My mother is one of twelve sisters, all but two still living in the county and the numbers of cousins and second cousins and quite likely third cousins, defies mathematics. This golden wedding party was not only a celebration of a long marriage but an excuse for a family knees-up. We promised we would arrive by boat and we did. Riverside festival not withstanding we were committed.

Co-incidentally Maidstone is also significant for me in another way. The town was the home of the Rootes Group vehicle and engine manufacturers and of course the very place where *Starry Vere's* engines were manufactured. By a bizarre twist of fate we were to learn we had moored directly opposite the old riverside Tillet and Stevens factory, the company that produced the engines for Rootes. It was fascinating but terribly frustrating. All sign of Tillett and Stevens has long gone of course and the old Rootes Group headquarters, I remember seeing when I was a child, is now a large Peugeot dealer. I'd just love to know what happened to all those spare parts.

Party and reunion over we had a date in London. Back down the Medway, into the estuary and up the Thames, that was our hope. It started raining as we locked through at Allington and by the time we had reached Rochester we were very soggy. A dreadful grey sky, incessant rain and an equally dreary shipping forecast persuaded us that plan B had to come into play; we needed to find a railway station. Approaching the impressive span of the new railway viaduct, just before Rochester, we moored alongside the pontoons of Cuxton Marina; we had spotted a small railway station just a short walk from the river. The wooden pontoons were like ice, treacherous in their sodden state and once on terra firma, well that was anything but firm, just sticky mud. The station proved to be no more than a deserted halt and, true to form, information regarding the possibility of a train passing through was distinctly lacking. Janet managed to attract the attention of a signal-box keeper who imparted the bad news that trains stopping at this spot were few and far between and even if one chanced by we would have to change a number of times to reach the capital. The other side of the river, in reach of Rochester, was where we needed to be. Evening gloom was well and truly descending as we trudged in our sodden state back to *Starry Vere*. I pressed the port engine starter button and was met by no more than a depressing click. Pressed again, the same pathetic sound, just what we needed. This had never happened before but of course these little inconveniences always pick their time. Down into the engine room, soggy trousers clinging to my cold legs, Oh the joys of boating! The wiring seemed ok; everything still attached. The battery was fine; we had been running no more than twenty minutes earlier. Perhaps the starter was jammed? I remember from early car owning days once or twice having to put my elderly cars in gear and then rock backwards and forwards to free the starter. Slight problem, you can't push a boat in quite the same way. Janet was now resigned to spending the night at Cuxton but as a last resort I grabbed a spanner and freed off the two large bolts that secure the starter motor to the flywheel casing, scientifically wriggled it about, applied a gentle tap here and there and tightened things up again. Back to the starter button and hey presto, we were back in business. Not sure how or why but Janet was pretty impressed and the starter has not repeated its misdemeanour since. Indeed a mystery but one in keeping with the mood of the moment. We let go and aimed downstream for the deep water mooring of Medway Bridge Marina. It was dark now, not a soul about and as we approached what we deduced to be the visitors pontoon the rain still poured. We'd had enough; an early start was required next day to locate the station. A hot meal and then to bed!

9

...whizzing and puffing, skirts all a-flow

"Drink up dad, it could be your last for some time!" Ben was precariously making his way toward us, a full pint glass in each hand, emerging from a bar packed with drinkers and littered with musical instrument cases. The clientele of *The Marquis of Granby* had spilled out onto the West End pavement, which on this muggy August evening was certainly the best place to be.

He was right of course. If all went to plan we would soon be on French soil, a land devoid of such congenial products as London Pride and Marsdon's Pedigree. I could manage the hardship, there are alternative French delights but I savoured the pint non-the less and enjoyed the moment; the excited post concert release, the banter and mutual congratulation for a job well done, between young, refreshingly unsullied musicians. It had been a marvellous concert.

Ben, understandably, was reluctant to tear himself away and it was only after a spirited dash through the still busy pavements that we managed to catch the last train from

Charing Cross down to Rochester. It was already after mid-night but of course London's 'theatre-land' was still full of life. The crowded train became progressively emptier and calmer as at each suburban stop passengers spilled out. It was one thirty in the morning when we finally pulled into Rochester station, the euphoria of London now well and truly evaporated. Three very tired people, the prospect of a mile and a half walk to the marina, a violin case and suitcase suddenly growing heavy and not a taxi in sight; we could do nothing but start marching. Thankfully, for tempers were beginning to fray, a cab came by and responded to our frantic attempts at being noticed. Within a couple of minutes we had been deposited in the silence of the marina but still with the problem of finding the boat. The previous morning we had left in some haste and in daylight. Aim for water, that seemed the best idea. We trudged through the eerie shapes of yachts and cruisers out on the hard toward the significant bulk of the old *Inner Dowsing* light-ship, now in retirement and serving as the marina clubhouse. This time of the morning it had long since been vacated but even bereft of its beacon it still stood as a trusty landmark, helping us find the slipway down to the river. We tramped along a very long, misty and murky pontoon, the night black as ink, but the familiar and comforting lines of *Starry Vere* emerged from the gloom and once aboard it was immediately into bed. The tide dictated we needed to leave at five thirty; perhaps three hours sleep if we were lucky!

I doubt if luck had much to do with it but we snatched what we could and by first light we were trying hard to enjoy a fine morning, cruising down the deserted River Medway. Ben was the lucky one. He surfaced a good three hours later when we were well into our coastal passage bound for North Foreland and Dover.

Studying the chart, this route didn't exactly fill me with eager anticipation. It's probably perfectly possible to cut the corner when exiting the Medway, back into the Thames estuary but I chose to religiously use the full length of the buoyed channel and make a turn to starboard once the Medway buoy had been reached. Call me cautious but even the Admiralty chart seems to give up on the area. Our turn from the main channel took us into a sea-area named on the chart as The Cant and then in brackets (*numerous pieces of wreckage*). Numerous pieces of wreckage...and with charted depths at best three metres. What good is that? Yes, OK, that means chart datum, a kind of worst-case scenario but thought provoking all the same. Spile buoy reached we entered Four Fathoms Channel. Again with a bracketed footnote, or is it a warning, or even a threat, (*at High Water*). What at high water? Four fathoms? A channel...? Spaniard East Cardinal buoy was our next waypoint and here we changed course for Hook Spit, heading in toward the coast. This area of seaway bears the delightful name Pudding Pan but again the men and women of the Admiralty add a vague caveat, (*cement boulders*). It's enough to give a poor mariner a nervous breakdown. We skirted the large sand bank, Margate Hook, via the disquietingly named Gore Channel - the consequence of cement boulders perhaps - and by 1030 we had made the sharp right turn into the English Channel, cruising about a mile off North Foreland. On our port side we now had to contend with the Goodwin Sands, ever shifting and again, according to the authorities at the Admiralty, "littered with wrecks". We were fortunate to be enjoying much improved weather and paying due care and attention to the ample buoyage we had no problem in approaching our goal of Dover; its ever growing proximity made apparent as the distinctive and famous white cliffs replaced an otherwise featureless coast-line.

We had been through the port many times over the years on cross-channel car ferries but I was looking forward to entering with *Starry Vere* what, in terms of sheer volume of traffic, must be one of the busiest ports there is. Entry and exit are very efficiently regulated. We called harbour control on the VHF radio and received instructions to enter by the east entrance and then stand on station to wait for an incoming vessel to cross our path. That vessel certainly appeared at speed, whizzing and puffing, skirts all a-flow, a cross channel hovercraft skimmed into the port, up the concrete ramp and after a gentle deflation deposited another cargo of holiday-makers in the UK with amazing celerity.

Dover now boasts comprehensive facilities for the cruising fraternity and as one would expect the marina contained yachts and powerboats on passage from many nations. Arriving at lunchtime we had the very welcome space to relax and recover after the excitement and sleep depravation of the previous thirty-six hours, with even a little time for exploration. What is striking about the place is the incessant stream of vehicular traffic heading to or from the ferries, to the point that crossing the road running outside the marina to reach the toilet and shower block was not only an inconvenience but also a perilous exercise.

France beckoned. Promptly next morning, feeling refreshed and encouraged by a good weather outlook, we fuelled up with the last of the low tax red diesel it would be possible to buy and turning our backs on the white cliffs, headed cross channel for Dieppe. The shortest most direct crossing is the twenty miles or so to Calais but our preference was to enter France via the River Seine at Le Havre and head straight for Paris. Fortune certainly smiled on us; weather and sea state could not have been kinder.

The Dover Strait is apparently the busiest shipping highway in the world. Highway is a very accurate analogy, for shipping passing through the strait is subject to a strictly enforced traffic separation zone, a kind of dual carriageway. Ships travelling up the strait, in a north-easterly direction, have a 'carriageway' nearer the French coast and conversely ships heading south-west, down the strait, must keep to a zone nearer the British coast. All this means traffic, cruising to France from Britain, or visa versa, has to cross directly through these shipping zones, or 'carriageways' and strict rules are in force to make a potentially tricky operation safer. The zone has to be crossed at ninety degrees, in theory at right angles to shipping on passage through the strait. We set our course to comply and passed within sight of the Varne light float. On a good day, such as this, with clear visibility, there shouldn't be a problem detecting and avoiding the shipping travelling at a surprising speed. I can imagine though if thick fog descended and particularly at night it would be a very different story. Radar is really essential but without doubt the age of the GPS has made procedures like this so much easier and safer. We knew exactly when the zone had been cleared and when to make the turn to starboard taking us down the French coast, keeping between two and three miles off in safe water.

It was a wonderfully easy and enjoyable passage, I don't think I have ever seen the sea so smooth, absolutely oily flat calm. *Starry Vere* cruised along very comfortably at her eight knots and by six in the evening we had entered our first French port. A celebration was definitely in order and once moored, with formalities attended to, we three intrepid sailors climbed the walkway out of the old harbour and headed for the nearest bar. In what seemed an amazingly short space of time we had journeyed from a busy pavement outside a British pub in the West End of London to the delights of a dockside French pavement café in Dieppe. Cheers! Salut! We deserved it!

The fabulous weather held for our final day at sea, giving us another comfortable and event-free cruise along the coast as far as the Seine estuary. This mighty river, initially a busy and important major route for shipping, would take us directly into the heartland of France and eventually offer us the most scenic and dramatic entrance into Paris that must be possible. First though an essential night in the marina of Le Havre, situated on the northern bank of the estuary. We had to plan for an optimum start on the trip up the river to the city of Rouen, a journey of well over a hundred kilometres which should really be achieved on one tide. Opportunities for an overnight stop before Rouen are virtually nil and given the rise and fall of the tide, not to mention the uncompromising speed of the large ships plying up and down the estuary, anchoring or securing to a bank-side mooring would be uncomfortable, if not dangerous. Not for the first time we had to do our homework to get it right!

The following day low water should have been around 1220 but either the flood was late in arriving or this time my calculations where not spot on. We left Le Havre at midday and made our way across the wide estuary to pick up the buoyage marking the entrance to the river but it was very apparent we were still pushing the considerable flow of the ebb as it streamed back out to sea. Progress for the first hour or so was rather slow. Still, it gave us time to view the new locked entrance into the historic port of Honfleur on the southern bank; plenty of time in fact as our momentum was only just in the forward direction. But at least when the tide did eventually turn we were in a good position to benefit from the exhilarating speed of the new flood.

One lesson quickly learnt was the need to keep a good watch astern. A couple of very large ships, also taking advantage of the new flood, crept up behind us and were certainly intent on overtaking regardless. The wash they created proved difficult to deal with in the confines of a river and on a later occasion I took to turning *Starry Vere* round to face the oncoming vessel and its subsequent tidal wave! Although tedious it offered perhaps a more comfortable solution. Time and tide…and these working ships wait for no man on the Seine.

As we left the open sea behind us and the wide-open flatness of the estuary gradually, almost imperceptibly, began to close in, we were transported into the new and very different experience of the inland waterways. It was to be some time before *Starry Vere* would be in salt water again.

10

...copious cursing and swearing

We made Rouen just as the sun was setting and secured to the undistinguished pontoons of the pleasure boat harbour, just upstream of Pont Corneille. Unfortunately we had deadlines to keep so an exploration of the city was not going to be possible. Ben had to leave us to return to London for concerts and Emma and Adam, already in France on a camping holiday, had planned a brief rendezvous in Paris. But the excitement of entering the capital by boat and spending a little time there *en famille* was to be compensation enough. We managed a brief night-time reconnoitre of the streets around the river but a true discovery of Rouen's undoubted charms would have to wait for another time.

Early the following morning I purchased the obligatory inland waterways licence from a nearby office of the French waterways authority, the *Voies Navigable de France*, or VNF and we pressed on up the river that grows more dramatically scenic every one of its two hundred and forty kilometres, plus six locks, to Paris. The potential problems of meeting sea going ships were forgotten and although commercial traffic in the form of large barges is still prevalent, the whole experience transformed into an easier going slow paced idyll. Magnificent cliffs line the river for much of the time and when they give way to flatter scenery the landscaped luxuriant gardens of fine houses and mini- châteaux provide glamour at the river's edge. It is a glamorous river, almost Rhine-like at times, with elegant prosperous bank-side communities offering picture post card images of traditional architecture with an historic castle or château overlooking all. Beautiful sunny weather made the three days we took to reach Paris extremely enjoyable, an absolute treat. We have a lovely photograph of Ben playing the violin on the foredeck as we cruised peacefully up the river.

Entering Paris was a wonderful and fantastic privilege. There must surely be no better way of approaching this magnificent city than by its 'front door' entrance of the Seine. It takes some time, the suburbs are extensive but this heightens the excitement. The river is central to the life of Paris; its commerce, culture, architecture, its raison d'etre…*bien sur* and the cruise through the outskirts was one of constant wonder and discovery. Complete communities live on the water and the endless variety of working barges, *peniches,* transformed into fashionable chic boat house dwellings, reflect the style one expects from the capital of style. We had a brilliant day, a blue sky quite dazzling in its almost Mediterranean concentrated vividness. We strained for our first glimpse of famous landmarks; the Eiffel tower, Statue of Liberty, Notre Dame. The closer we got to the centre so the frequent bridges became ever more elegant. Some of burnished white classical stone, others of gloriously painted and gilded iron. Famous names; Pont de la Concorde, Pont Royal, Pont Neuf. All the time the river awash with traffic; large commercial barges, intent on their work, busy *bateaux mouches*, water borne glass roofed coaches full of happy tourists enjoying the guided tour, at high speed. One hand on the helm the other grasping my camera trying to capture the scene, which in reality would only be successfully captured by the mind. Ben on the bow with his camera. Excitedly we encouraged each other to look one way then the other as landmarks passed by. We gestured and enthused, superlatives exhausted. The remarkable perspective of the Eiffel Tour when viewed from the river. There on the right the magnificent Musee d'Orsay, once the most opulent railway station ever... left the Palais du Louvre. Then Notre Dame, so disappointing when visited as part of a crush of sightseers but from our own private viewing area, at a perfect distance, *magnifique!!* It was over too soon but the busy Seine, in the middle of August, is not the place to linger. We left the river via the ecluse de l'Arsenal and entered the relative calm of the city's port de plaisance; exhilarated!

Not dissimilar to London's St Catherine Dock the Paris Arsenal, as the main pleasure boat mooring is known, is wonderfully situated for experiencing the city at close quarters. Within sight of the Place de la Bastille most of the great attractions of Paris are so easy to reach, some on foot and others further afield but the metro system works. We also enjoyed just walking out of the port and into the local shops to buy our daily bread, experiencing Paris as a local. We were locals of course and for one week our home *was* in the city. Emma and Adam arrived in time to enjoy an evening with Ben before he departed. The weather was great, very hot, and we ate *al fresco* on the foredeck, enjoying the meal and the company well into the night. In fact it was so hot Emma and Adam took to sleeping under the stars.

It was time for Ben to return to London using Eurostar and while he was pulling together both his belongings and his thoughts it dawned on him he was missing a passport. Leaving London directly after the concert and then entering France by small boat he had completely overlooked the fact it would be needed and as has been our experience, he had not been asked to produce it. One would think travelling between Paris and London minus a passport, in a modern Europe, shouldn't be an insurmountable problem so off he went on the metro; we weren't quite sure if he would be back.

Later that day, thankfully by telephone from London, he related his amusing passage back through British passport control. Arriving at the Eurostar terminal in Paris he thought it best to own up before buying a ticket. Firstly he needed to explain to the French police the circumstances surrounding his arrival in Paris and despite sarcastic comments to the effect that perhaps he should return to England by boat, he was allowed to travel. So he made it back to the UK but then there was British immigration control to contend with. Once again Ben explained his situation to an official whose first apparent reaction was to doubt his story. I can just imagine how Ben felt. The official started to dig deeper, how could he be sure Ben was a British citizen? Perhaps a question or two to prove citizenship... *"can you tell me who won the cup final in 1959?"* A wind up, a passport officer with a sense of humour. I bet Ben didn't know it was Nottingham Forest!

Emma and Adam also left to fly back to the UK and so once again we were just two, ready to continue our voyage. During the weeklong stay in Paris we had moored next to a British boat, *Saxton Chieftain*, with owners Andy and Barbara. They too were heading south and having shared a bottle or three during the week we decided to head out of the Arsenal together. In continuing fine weather we locked through to re-enter the river, a left turn and then on, up the upper Seine, cruising in convoy through the city suburbs. After less than five kilometres the waterway forks, the River Marne to the left and the Seine continuing to the right, our chosen route. A couple more kilometres and we reached the first lock, appropriately called Port a l'Anglais. Perhaps *les Anglais* come in for special attention at this lock as the keeper or eclusier, intent on giving us a full demonstration of his authority, barked down from the open window of his high level control point with instructions to attend him with our ship's papers…*tout suite*! Once satisfied all was in order he mellowed a little and even offered us the good advice to keep to the back of the lock if possible when cruising up-stream; there is far less turbulence as the lock fills. These are large commercial locks and usually no mercy is shown to pleasure craft, *plaisance*, as we are known, that have to be tolerated. We didn't quite make the next lock, forgetting that seven is closing time but finding a quayside mooring was not a problem.

A further day and a half of relaxed easy cruising brought us to Montereau and the junction with the River Yonne, an equally scenic waterway but with one major difference that made our passage less idyllic and at times quite a challenge. I have completely failed to ascertain why the locks on the Yonne were built with sloping sides, *bajoyers inclines*, as the French pilot book nonchalantly describes them. The very words send me into a hot sweat. We approached the ecluse Cannes 17, the first Yonne lock. Picture the scene, you enter the lock and find yourself in a chamber where both walls, either side, drop down into the water at a slant, creating a kind of 'V' shape. The boat has to stay in the middle because below the water line the sloping walls make the area in which to float progressively narrower. Getting too close to either side means the boat will invariably make contact with solid stone. But even more serious, particularly on a twin-engined boat such as *Starry Vere*, is the fact that propellers and rudders become very, very, vulnerable. So we are sitting in the centre of the lock, wondering how to make fast to a bollard some distance away at the top of each side of the 'V'. Unless you are an expert with the lasso shore-side help is absolutely essential but usually the only person around is a disinclined lock keeper, loath to venture down from his control point. Then the sluices are opened to fill the lock. Not a helpful gentle flow but a torrent that sends the boat in all directions. It became immediately apparent tying to a shore side bollard is not the ideal solution. Such is the distance from boat to bollard that when the boat is thrust backward by the ingress of water, the necessary length of the rope has the undesired effect of pulling the boat into the side. *Starry Vere* weighs almost twenty tons and trying to fend off with a boat hook was only marginally successful. That first encounter with the *inclines* was a baptism of fire, the sound of metal on stone is one of my most enduring memories. We did work out a strategy for subsequent locks, with some success, but coping with what the Yonne threw at us was not one of our triumphs… and it got worse.

We were now well away from the environs of Paris, in fact the Yonne has some quite wild and remote stretches.

We spent a night at the ecluse Port-Renard 14 giving us the opportunity to wander around a local area very quiet and deserted. This lock is at a junction where the river is left to wind away on its natural course, through isolated woods and fields, leaving the navigable channel along a narrow but straight by-pass canal with a lock at each end.

The ecluse St Martin 10, just a couple of kilometres before the city of Sens, was probably the scene of our worst experience during the whole trip through France. Yet another lock, we had done so many that even the *inclines* were becoming routine. So many times Janet and I have re-run the events of St Martin 10 over in our minds but as is usual with disasters, well a near disaster, it happened so quickly and without warning. All had been normal, we entered the lock still in convoy with *Saxton Chieftain*, they were ahead of us. The lock filled, the gates opened, *Saxton Chieftain* drew out and then for some unknown reason I broke my own golden rule and got off the boat, leaving Janet on board. I suspect it was a little breezy and the boat started to drift away from the side. I remember asking Janet to just push the gear levers forward to engage forward motion, trying to keep the boat straight. The next thing I knew the boat was heading backwards at some speed toward the lock gates. Then forward heading toward the lock wall with me pushing the bow trying to fend it off. Panic set in, I was shouting instructions to Janet who was struggling with the controls up on the outside helm position. I have this fleeting vision of the lock keeper standing at the other end of the lock, jaw hitting the floor, wondering what on earth was going on. *Starry Vere* seemed to have a mind of her own, a bucking bronco in a rodeo perhaps something close. It was a very unpleasant few seconds, for that is probably all it was. It seemed like a lifetime. Sanity eventually prevailed and when we regained some semblance of control the problem became apparent. A mooring rope had slipped off the starboard stern quarter and very quickly wrapped itself around the prop. A moment of slackness, in fact a mortal sin and we paid for it. Fortunately, apart from some minor paint loss, no damage was sustained except we had a debilitated boat. I felt a bit of a twit for causing so much mayhem and as we finally limped out of the lock on one engine we passed a rather bemused eclusier. *"pas probleme"*, was all I could feebly manage.

So we had a mooring rope well and truly wrapped around the propeller and quite probably shaft as well. That was the bad news. The good news? How fortunate we were, just no further than a kilometre from the lock sits a boatyard. Even better, a boat yard run by an English family; Evans Marine. It has to be said under any other circumstances we would have cruised passed Evans Marine without a second thought, except perhaps a comment about the ramshackle mess of boats and barges in various states of repair, or was it decay. We now have a completely different perspective. Help was needed and we certainly got it. It may have been at a leisurely pace, for although English by birth the Evans family have very competently absorbed the working practices of the French, particularly it being lunch-time when we limped into their midst. We waited and waited but finally lunch was completed and when it happened it certainly happened in style. I reversed *Starry Vere* between the collection of moored craft, up to the bank-side and next to a business-like crane. An audience gathered from nowhere and believe it or not, wine bottles were opened and glasses passed around the growing band of spectators. One of the three Evans brothers manoeuvred the enormous crane as near as possible to the water's edge and a sling was passed under the boat's stern. Help and advice came from all directions, the afternoon was taking on a carnival atmosphere. The crane roared into life and *Starry Vere's* rump lifted out of the water, her nose digging down into the mud. A small dingy was summoned and an Evans brother, I never did learn his name, very precariously, almost laying in the dingy, grappled under the boat with a sharp knife attacking the task of cutting rope from prop and shaft. Synthetic rope when subject to extreme friction, even under water, tends to weld together and accompanied by copious cursing and swearing, in French and English, the offending specimen was removed. The spectacle went on for some time but inch-by-inch one of our best mooring ropes was cut free.

The peace and quiet of the quay at Sens that evening was heaven. What a day! We had only travelled about fifteen kilometres but it felt like a major voyage; a bottle of vin rouge was never so welcome. The following morning it all seemed like a bad dream.

We recuperated in Sens for a couple of days and it turned out to be a very fine place in which to linger. Mooring is easy and very convenient for the city dominated by not only the oldest but the largest gothic cathedral in France. Outside and in it is quite extraordinary.

Saxton Chieftain pressed on, Andy and Barbara were keen to get further south before the autumn set in. We… we had a phone-call, our property management agents. It was bound to be bad news, it always is. There is never a call saying Oh, Mr Nabarro, the tenants love the flat so much they have offered to pay more rent. No, a phone call means a problem and this had the makings of a serious one, the bogey of the Yonne had struck again. Before leaving the UK we had tackled the 'simple' task of converting our family home into two self-contained flats. It appeared the ground floor flat had developed an infestation of some description, something to do with mushrooms growing on the front room carpet! An expert was to be summoned and we would be informed of the prognosis.

In the meantime we bade farewell to Sens and continued our exploration of the Yonne as it meanders through gentle countryside and the very pleasant communities of Villneuve sur Yonne and Joigny. Unfortunately we were preoccupied, waiting for the next phone-call that could only bring unpleasant news and sure enough when it came it certainly was bad; a severe case of dry rot. It sounded serious as well as potentially expensive; we could see no option other than travelling back to the UK to supervise remedial work. Although this was at best a boring inconvenience, fortune did smile on us in her own perverse way. Not a great deal further up the river, close to the small community of Migenne and the junction with the Canal de Bourgogne, we found yet another boatyard with an English owner. Joe Parfitt's yard, a possible solution to the headache of where to safely leave *Starry Vere*.

We didn't know it but proprietor Joe was on holiday. The riverside moorings, although looking tidier and better organised than the Evan's yard at Sens, non-the less were congested with the usual variety of barges and smaller craft. Among them was a pert cruiser sporting the red ensign and as we drew alongside the owner, English spoken but not English, popped out to greet us, or perhaps it was to see what we were up to. After initial pleasantries I explained our predicament and the urgent need to find a safe mooring for perhaps a couple of weeks. A yard employee came along to help. Our new found ally took charge of the situation and in a display of what could only be described as colonial arrogance proceeded to explain our needs in very pedantic and very loud English. Janet and I couldn't believe it. The chap left to manage the yard, obviously French, had no English but was expected to understand when spoken to in this way. It was embarrassing and demeaning yet of course amusing, the stuff of TV comedy programmes, Monty Python coming to mind!

All was organised, I'm not sure how, but we were to remain rafted to our 'colonial' friend's boat for the night; the following morning he would be departing. We were invited on board for a beer. The weather was hot, we had become very close neighbours, it was impossible to say no. Once aboard introductions naturally took place and at this point I will refrain from naming names but it was apparent we had failed to register who our host actually was. A failing on our part it has to be said as we were informed politely yet emphatically he was... a world famous yacht designer... no I won't name names just in case he is world famous. We had no idea, but come to that he had never heard of me either! His charming wife also turned out to be a bit of a celebrity in the boating magazine world and for an hour or so we drank our host's beer whilst being subjected to the full gravity of his importance to the worldwide marine fraternity. They departed the next day and left us to the peace and tranquillity of Joe Parfitt's otherwise rather modest boat yard.

Sadly, very sadly, we had to depart too. A regular train service ran from Migennes to Paris and from there Eurostar to London and the Midland Mainline to Nottingham. We left Migennes at eight in the morning and by five o'clock in the afternoon we were back in our flat. It all seemed as if we had never been away but for one lingering image. As the train drew out of Migennes station the line crosses the Yonne, the bridge overlooking Joe Parfitt's yard. There sat *Starry Vere*, our home, forlornly tied to the outside of a barge. We hadn't a clue when we would return.

11

...nothing like a rat-hole

The month of September was a trial, to put it mildly. Although it was great to be able to catch up with family and friends, most of the month we felt imprisoned in our upstairs flat whilst downstairs dry rot specialists, builders, plumbers, insurance claim assessors, came – sometimes and went - often. The tenants, who were wonderfully understanding and patient, also had to endure the upheaval. Carpets removed, floorboards lifted, plaster chopped off some walls down to the bare brick, doors removed, dust and mess everywhere. Then nasty chemicals injected and painted. At first the insurance company didn't want to know. The total bill was to be thousands, we wanted them to know...and pay up. The breakthrough came when the plumber declared that a leaking central heating pipe below the floor had caused the rot. This changed everything, we were covered for water leaks; I could have kissed him but thought better of it. Wonder of wonders, the insurers eventually agreed but not before a considerable hiatus that kept us in suspense to the end. After four weeks we were aching to get back on that train.

With some relief we spotted *Starry Vere* as we crossed the bridge drawing into Migennes station. Within ten minutes we were on board, throwing open doors and windows and revelling in our return with brilliant sunshine a wonderful bonus. Before moving into the canal we had contemplated visiting the beautiful old cathedral city of Auxerre, just a little further up the river and even discussed the possibility of wintering there until the following spring. But now we were back we had a strong urge to be off, heading south for the winter like a couple of migrating birds just released from a cage.

Once into the extensive inland waterway system of northern France if, like most dreamers, the focus of those rêves is the Mediterranean, then we are presented with a choice of three main routes. All converge onto the river Saône in Burgundy and then follow a common course down this quite stunning river to Lyon where from then on it's into the very different downhill rush south of the mighty Rhône. Each alternate route has its benefits but we liked the sound of the canal de Bourgogne. We had read of its beauty and history; the thought of traversing Burgundy was an attractive proposition, for of course we were seeking vineyards although much to our disappointment we were to see virtually none. Hard to believe, but despite its promising name this canal is not the route for wine. It is the route for locks however; we were to face a staggering one hundred and eighty-nine during the course of its two hundred and forty-two kilometre length.

September was almost past when we left the River Yonne and locked through into the canal, with only another one hundred and eighty-eight to go! We sensed a new adventure shaping up after cruising the rivers and immediately on our first French canal a number of minor worries surfaced. Would there be enough depth? These bridges look very low... and the locks are so narrow. The whole experience was obviously man-made, more restricted and contrived. In many ways a canal is similar to a railway line, with embankments, cuttings and that feeling of entering and leaving communities via the back door. Our pace was certainly to be slower but with this adjustment came a bonus of time to observe and enjoy plus, negotiating so many locks day after day was to hone our skills in that department. Rather like practising scales on a musical instrument, repetitive, sometimes monotonous but to succeed, essential. We were now constantly climbing; the summit of this canal, at nearly four hundred metres above sea level, is the highest you can sail a boat in France.

Being in the midst of nature it became very noticeable how summer was sliding into autumn. Sadly the sun had deserted us and now depressing leaden skies and incessant rain greeted us each morning. Still, I mused, it should ensure we are unlikely to run out of water in which to float; a phenomenon, I had read, not unknown in this canal, particularly toward the end of a dry summer.

Once we were happy in our routine we called Andy and Barbara of *Saxton Chieftain* to catch up on their progress. It was obvious they were already enjoying the Mediterranean with irritating tales of swimming in the sea and lounging on a beach. But one piece of news we were pleased to receive was a hot tip for a winter mooring; an inland port on the River Lez near Montpellier, evidently very secure and with very reasonable mooring fees. Barbara passed on the phone number and we worked out our spiel in French. With a limited linguistic skill telephone calls are certainly the most problematic form of communication. Having drawn the short straw it was down to me to make the call, albeit with some trepidation. It made me realise how dependant we are on hands, eyes and other forms of sign language but I proudly managed to get past my opening gambit before the put down, *"perhaps we should carry on in English"* came the reply. Relief of course but a mental note, must do better! It was worth the effort, for with a mooring secured for the winter months we had peace of mind.

After eight leisurely days and a total distance covered of only one hundred and fifteen kilometres (the books are right when they say allow three weeks) we awarded ourselves a rest day in Venarey les Laumes before tackling the final haul up to the summit at Pouilly en Auxois. Fifty-five locks in the space of thirty-nine kilometres and staggeringly, thirty-seven of these in the first twelve kilometres, after leaving Venarey. Generally the locks are man-matic with simple yet effectively engineered machinery dating back to the nineteenth century and although eclusiers are on hand to oversee groups of locks, we are expected to do our bit. It can be a tiring experience jumping on and off the boat, particularly coupled with copius amounts of fresh air but none the less a great way to keep fit.

Traffic on this particular canal, as it is on most of the smaller rural canals, is now almost one hundred percent pleasure boating. Relegated to history are the days when this would have been a busy scene of commerce, with hundreds of commercial barges constantly weaving an industrial route through this very rural setting. No romantic images then, for despite the beauty of the workplace it was undoubtedly a tough existence. Live-a-board extended families lived in the close quarters of one aft cabin and before the days of engine power not only horses were employed to pull the barges along the canals but children and womenfolk. It must have been a close-knit society with families of lock keepers, *eclusiers*, each resident in a tied cottage found at every lock, also forming an integral part of this industry.

These days many of the cottages are boarded up and derelict, or occasionally let by the authorities to individuals seeking a tranquil existence. The diminishing band of eclusiers still employed to work the system now service whole flights of locks and race up and down the canal towpath in this pursuit on noisy mopeds or motor scooters. They certainly are a different breed to those on the more commercial rivers and as we were assigned our eclusier for half a day or more we had time to observe some interesting characters at work. We often offered tea or coffee, giving us chance to socialise and exercise our limited French. In particular we have fond memories of one eclusier who refused all offers of refreshment, insisting it would spoil his lunch. When he returned for the afternoon session it was obvious what kind of lunch he didn't want to spoil. Now with a glint in his eye and an unsteadiness mounting his moped it brightened up our afternoon's progress through yet more locks. With the policy of automation rampant this would be the end of a way of life.

Admittedly it was well out of the main season but still we found the dearth of other boats a little disconcerting. There are a number of large hotel barges plying along certain sections, dredging as they push through the shallow canal but how long will the French government continue to fund the extensive staffing and maintenance costs necessary to keep the canal open? There have certainly been scare stories of closure in the past and what a tragic loss it would be.

After almost two weeks we reached the *'crowning glory of the canal'*, as Derek Bowskill describes it, the summit tunnel at Pouilly en Auxois. With a straight-line rather romantic length of three thousand, three hundred and thirty-three metres, it is certainly an astonishing feat of engineering. Andy and Barbara had told us all about it on the phone, along with a word of advice, *"don't go and look at it before you go through, it's a rat hole"*. Well of course with advice like that we just had to go and look. We took an evening stroll and sauntered alongside the narrow approach cutting, beautifully lined with trees. The depth and the eventual severity of the cutting through the dark rock give the impression of a tunnel way before the tunnel actually starts. The first glimpse of the entrance must be from a distance of no more than five hundred metres and naturally Andy and Barbara's description was a mere embellishment, the entrance looks nothing like a rat-hole. *Mouse-hole* would be more like it! It is frighteningly small. Although we knew that many boats had been through before us, at that moment we found it hard to imagine *Starry Vere* would fit.

OK, check the measurements; height above the waterline, this is the crucial dimension. True, when we came through the final lock at Pouilly the lady eclusiére had not seemed concerned. We had been asked to demonstrate our spotlight and horn, show that we had life jackets and that our navigation lights were in good order. But she seemed quite relaxed about our size; surely she must have seen many boats pass through... mustn't she? As a precaution though, I decided to take down the windscreen. Apart from that, the head had to rule the heart; on paper we would fit.

The following morning, a chilly and damp Sunday, I knocked on the eclusiére's cottage door, as previously instructed, to get the all clear. There appeared to be a well used routine where the eclusiére rings through to her counter-part at la Lochére, the other side of the tunnel, to make sure no other traffic will be passing through from the other direction. Overtaking or passing is impossible so a strict one-way system is imposed, which is good news. We got the all clear… the tunnel was ours.

I helmed from the outside position; Janet sat up-front on the bow. We advanced down the cutting, the same view as the previous evening, we would surely never fit. Nearer, and I called for Janet's opinion. She was about ten metres further forward than me and lower down. Her reply was confident and reassuring. Only later did Janet admit her misgivings but she thought at the time I needed a positive approach! We must have been no more than fifteen metres away when I realised the tunnel actually becomes lower just beyond the entrance. Hell's teeth! But there was no turning back and our modest speed needed to be maintained to ensure steerage. There was certainly no room for error.

Then we were in, enveloped in darkness, just the glare of our spotlight illuminating the ancient vaulted brickwork and wonderfully visible, in the far distance, a white pinhole of light. The tunnel really was dead straight. Once the initial excitement had calmed we could begin to enjoy the experience, although such was my concentration in keeping the boat on a straight course I emerged with a splitting headache and shivering with cold. There was very little headroom to spare and even with my modest height the arched roof seemed very close to my head.

It is though quite remarkable. The tunnel first went into use in 1842 and the brickwork, appearing to form a complete circle with the canal surface its diameter, remains amazingly sound and smooth. It took fifty minutes to make the passage and when we popped out into daylight it was into an even more dramatic cutting than the one we had left at the other end. It's all downhill from now on, only seventy-six more locks to go before the river Saône and the descent starts with a bang; a staircase of eight consecutive locks in the space of just over two kilometres.

Leaving the tunnel we were now into some remote terrain with communities small and infrequent. Well-wooded, with spectacular scenery, the canal hugs the curvaceous diminutive River Ouche all the way to the city of Dijon. Very attractive you might think. Well, yes, but there was a draw back. For the first time in living memory we were unable to purchase bread…in France. I wandered around deserted streets in a number of small hamlets but there was not a sign of a boulangerie. A friendly eclusier took pity and sold us a loaf, straight from her freezer!

The weather was not helpful either. We were experiencing some very low atmospheric pressure and on the 11th October our barometer dropped to nine hundred and fifty-eight millibars. I'm no expert but this seemed pretty low to me and the result was high winds and continuing torrential rain. Lock after lock in sodden clothes, wet and slippery ropes, slimy stone walls, the experience starts to pall, particularly when you receive phone-calls from friends who are still extolling the virtues of lazy sunny days swimming in the Med. We pressed on, keen to reach the better weather but wary also of the potential for flooding after so much rain. No more than a lunch break in Dijon, which was a shame in many ways and after eighteen days of canal life we reached St Jean de Losne and the exit into the River Saône. Our timing was poor though, lunchtime, a sacred not to be meddled with mealtime in France and coupled with the incessant rain this was no incentive at all for a reluctant eclusier to drag himself out of the warm and dry. Patiently we waited and when he finally arrived, full of smiles and "mon dieu... oh, what terrible weather", we were just grateful to escape the canal and enter the grown-up world of the river.

12

...never has a man washed so many bras!!

The small town of Saint Jean de Losne is beautifully situated on the banks of the Saône and a major crossroad for the boating world with an importance and reputation amongst boat people, both commercial and pleasure, far greater than its actual size should warrant. It holds a fortuitous strategic position, for not only does the canal de Bourgogne converge here, just four kilometres further north the canal du Rhône-au-Rhin meets the river and another day's cruising upstream would bring us to the junction with the canal de la Marne a la Saône. Boat traffic heading south, from virtually the whole of northern Europe, has to pass this way and St Jean, with extensive moorings, fuel barge, boat yards, well-equipped chandleries and three well stocked supermarkets, has become an important staging post. The result is a fluid melting pot of nationalities, ages and social backgrounds, united in satisfying their migratory urge south, whether it be en route or sometimes on the less exciting return leg, perhaps back to reality and often a need to sell.

But there does seem to be an inherent danger in the place, a certain magnetism that has the power to snare an innocent boater who, merely by stopping to revital and repair, can be seduced into hanging up their sea legs and putting down roots, even to the extent of forsaking their boats for the permanence of bricks and mortar. And the result? Well this undistinguished, ordinary, one-main-street-of-a-place, has become home to an unusual mixed community of eclectic incomers living alongside the long-term locals who appear to be completely indifferent to their mix of neighbours and the undoubted prosperity they bring to the area.

Up to around fifty years ago the sepia scene at St Jean would have been one of a riverside quay packed with commercial barges. Imagine each barge housing an extended family; children of all ages climbing over the boats, perhaps swimming and fooling in the water; laundry, recently washed in the river hanging over a mast to dry and the men, whilst waiting in strict rotation for their next load to be dispensed from a riverside office called the Bourse, spending their days in one of a parade of bars lining the quay. Even though the commercial barging industry in these parts has all but disappeared the bars that have survived and like most French towns there are still quite a few, still seem to hold on to that lost era. The ever-growing influx of pleasure boaters during the summer months has provoked a commercial spark with tables and parasols erected al fresco on what is a superb riverside position. But wander in for a beer during the darker parts of the year, peer through a smoky atmosphere, past the nicotine yellow walls, to the bar supported by three or four local men and all that is missing from a bygone age are the crowds of animated, pastis drinking, bargees.

Leaving the Burgundy Canal we nosed out into the wide fast flowing river, took a turn to port and headed upstream under the road bridge toward the excellent quay. We were lucky to find a mooring, taking one of the last available spots and it was here we enjoyed one of those very brief encounters, a real St Jean de Losne moment; interesting folk you immediately feel you could spend more time with.

I noticed a yellow, yes bright yellow motor-sailor, slowly passing the line of moored boats, searching for a mooring. The quay was full, it was of course still raining, the light was failing fast and so with a benevolent heart I beckoned them to raft alongside us for the night. During our introductory chat, as wet ropes were thrown across and made fast, we learnt they were Norwegians heading for their winter mooring in Torrevieja, southern Spain. Bearing in mind it was now well into October my immediate thought was they were leaving it rather late. It became even more interesting when we discovered their boat was home made and they had crossed the Atlantic... twice. Mentally swallowing a large slice of humble pie it was clear they probably did know what they were doing.

The following morning our neighbours were up promptly and had departed before we had even surfaced. The previous evening they intimated they hoped to cover something like a hundred kilometres during the following day and that was the last we saw of them, even though we set off close on their heels. We made a total of ninety-seven kilometres ourselves, it was not hard to cover such distances with the river running high and exhilaratingly fast. When we pulled out of the main channel at Chalon sur Saône with a view to buying fuel from the marina, the strength of the flow became very apparent. It was tricky coming alongside the fuel pontoon and considerably trickier leaving it. No time for feint hearts, the river in such spate gives only one opportunity to make a move and only decisive action with the throttles kept us away from the many moored boats. I was relieved to get back into the main stream.

We gave up chasing Norwegians at the pretty town of Tournus and decided to moor on the excellent pontoons. Strong mooring ropes were essential; the debris coming down the river was tremendous, sometimes whole trees. During the night we were subjected to constant and unnerving bumping and scrapping as all kinds of detritus floated by.

The following morning brought no respite, if anything the state of the river was deteriorating. We cracked on at a truly cracking pace; occasionally the GPS registered ten knots over the ground even though we were doing no more than six through the water. As we zoomed under the road bridge at Montmerle sur Saône we noticed a decent looking mooring pontoon on our port side that must have been fairly new as it receives no mention in the pilot book. A good size yacht was already alongside but there was ample room for us. *Starry Vere* was reluctant to slow down; she was on the crest of a wave and by the time I had manoeuvred round to face the flow we were way past the pontoon. Our engines were certainly called upon to work for the first time that day and stemming the current we clawed our way back to the pontoon. Drawing alongside the yacht our healthy roar must have sounded the alert for a couple of folk jumped out to offer help and very welcome it was with the difficult circumstances. They spoke the New Zealand brand of English and within five minutes we were secure and drinking tea aboard the yacht *Wild Bird*, another one of those marvellous boating liaisons where the rapport is instant.

Colin and Marian plus teenage daughters Wendy and Joanne had been living aboard for seven years and very slowly sailing around the world. Their story was fascinating; the girls of course had grown up on the yacht and alongside a fantastic education just through experience they were receiving a formal component via a correspondence course system. A couple of more balanced civilised teenagers you could not wish to meet, indeed the whole family were just great friendly and open people. Like us they were heading for the Mediterranean from the UK and by coincidence they had spent the previous winter in Ipswich. Just so much to talk about.

The still rising level and increasing flow of the Saône was a concern to both crews but we agreed that if at all possible the city of Lyon, less than fifty kilometres further, would be a far better place to see out the flood if we had to. By three o'clock the following afternoon we were safely moored on the quai Marechal-Joffre, upstream of the Bureau d'Affretement on the left bank. With busy road traffic passing alongside and a couple of rail and road bridges directly ahead it isn't exactly the most peaceful mooring but very well situated for a little sight-seeing in this, the second city of France.

Lyon is built on the confluence of the rivers Saône and Rhône, "historical cross-roads of Western Europe", as the guidebook says. History there certainly is, particularly the Gallo-Roman and medieval old city rising up from the river on the right-bank, the quarter of Fourviere. A couple of times we climbed up through the old narrow streets, edged by their Renaissance town houses. On, further and higher, there's a complete Roman amphitheatre that has found new life as a performance venue, everything from boxing to opera. Then at the very top the spectacular Notre Dame de Fourviere with a most brilliant viewpoint offering a superb panorama over the river to the city. Lyon is also a major commercial, industrial and cultural centre, obviously extraordinarily rich in diversity and opportunity. As usual we only scratched the surface of what the place has to offer but realistically that is all we can hope for as we go about our peripatetic way.

After a couple of days the river started to abate and we felt happier about embarking on the challenge that is the mighty Rhône. One of Europe's great rivers, a key communications route since Roman times, it was always a notoriously problematic navigation. To say that it has now been tamed would show a complacency asking for trouble. A vast programme of works begun in 1933 and only completed in 1980 set about harnessing rather than taming and the river is now navigable for most of the year. Probably the main benefit to the mariner is the ability to linger and explore. Once it was a dash, running the gauntlet of the river and often only possible with the help of a Rhône pilot. That has certainly changed and the dramatic beauty and character of the Rhône valley, plus the obvious and sometimes not so subtle change in climate as the Mediterranean south is approached, can now be savoured. We have a vivid memory of cruising for an afternoon with the distant Alps clearly visible on our port side and the mountains of the Ardeche on the starboard.

Spectacular man-made creations, built to cope with the natural spectacle of the dramatically falling river level, are twelve enormous locks. Not only do they make navigation

The vast chamber of a Rhône lock

possible, each lock is part of a hydroelectric plant, harnessing the enormous fall of water to provide something like a fifth of France's electricity needs. They were certainly a completely different experience to anything we had met before. Travelling down-stream you enter high; each chamber is vast, one hundred and ninety-five metres long by twelve metres wide, with an anonymous eclusier working all from his high level, highly technical, control tower. Mooring is easy to the floating bollards and then, when the water falls, silently and gently, we descend for what seems forever into the gloom of a cathedral-like space. The enormous guillotine gate lifts in front of us and we cruise out, back into the sunshine. These locks are a spectacular feat of engineering and an awe-inspiring experience, particularly when you have the chamber all to yourself.

We took four leisurely days, aided by a swift current, to cruise virtually the length of the river to Arles, the last major centre before meeting the sea and even though it was late October we were now back in T-shirts and shorts. Our final stop before Arles, at the tiny village of St Etienne des Sorts, was one to relish. The community is to be lauded for providing a splendid two boats at a squeeze modern pontoon mooring but we pondered, why? On initial exploration we found nothing in the small hamlet other than a boulangerie with erratic opening hours and a small café. Or so we thought. Exploring further on our trusty fold-ups we discovered the major asset of the village and quite probably its raison d'être, a cave co-operative, a wine making factory, serving many of the small grape growers in the area. True, there was nothing too fantastic about the building. In a region bristling with superior wine establishments this was modest to the point of tatty. It was, we discovered, the product, the Côte de Rhône that was worthy of the accolade 'fantastic'. Catching first sight of the cave we screeched to a halt, the smell of burning rubber rising from our brake blocks as we pulled to an emergency stop. A definitely no frills establishment it turned out to be, always a promising sign and with day-to-day work obviously on-going.

A young man spotted us lurking with intent. Our request for a degustation, a tasting, was positively received and an array of bottles, plus tasting glasses, were enthusiastically assembled around the obligatory up-turned barrel. We tasted and we enjoyed enormously, particularly the aptly named *Cuveé Mariner* and certainly wished to purchase but our order promptly doubled when the proprietor dropped his trump card and offered to deliver to the boat. What an effective sales ploy! Later we lamented the opportunity lost to purchase more, for the wine was very good and at an amazing price.

Reaching Arles we knew we had reached the Mediterranean. The sun shone for us as it must have for Van Gogh, whose past presence pervades the town. Even in late October the light was brilliant. We revelled for four days in weather and history, during which time *Wild Bird* arrived and rafted alongside. A very democratic and modern crew are the *Wild Bird* bunch. Each takes a turn to do the washing, usually in a tub out on deck. In Arles it was Colin's turn, which he undertook with much grace and the wry observation, living with three women never has a man washed so many bras!!

Our winter mooring, booked for Lattes on the River Lez, ran from the beginning of November so we really needed to move on. A short return back up the Rhône was necessary, only about three kilometres but more than enough against the strong current. Then a turn to port into the Petit Rhône and such a very different experience. The whole feel was more enclosed with the banks of this distinctly narrower waterway lined with trees and heavy undergrowth; you could almost imagine crocodiles in this more exotic atmosphere. The Petit Rhône, as its name implies, is an offspring of the main river. It runs down through the famous wetlands of the Camargue and eventually reaches the sea, although exit by boat here is not possible. We were aiming for the St Gilles lock that would deliver us into the canal du Rhône a Sete for the final stage of our voyage before the winter break.

This canal is remarkable for it's straightness along a flat coastal plain, which initially forms part of the Camargue and ends at the Etang du Thau, near the port of Sete. Exiting the lock it was amazing how we were suddenly in Camargue country. Flat wide open expanses of marshland, thick with reeds, very few trees and an enormous blue sky. Grey Herons and rarer White Egrets, with their distinguishing yellow feet, feeding in the shallows at the edge of the canal. All we needed now, to complete the picture-postcard images, were a few pink flamingos, white horses or black bulls… prophetic thoughts as we were to experience Camargue wild life at close quarters sooner than we imagined.

Not too far on and we moored at a simply delightful bank-side spot, just outside the unassuming Camargue village of Gallician. Unassuming it may have looked but this is frontier country; hunting is a major activity and as we were to discover very vividly, the Camargue version of the bullfight is a popular and traditional spectacle. The village was easy to explore, basically a one street place with a central area, not exactly a square but a road junction with a café-bar creating a kind of focal point. As usual we had a nose for local produce and sniffed out the local cave co-operative and its excellent *Costieres de Nime*. Later, quite by accident as it was not immediately obvious, we came across an independent wine producer, *Mas du Notaire*, tucked away behind an old stone archway. I'm glad we made this find, the wine was absolutely first rate and as usual at a price we still find hard to understand.

Strolling down the 'main street' we were intrigued by various notices stuck to the lampposts. In French, English and German, they seemed to warn of an imminent event and its potential danger. The translation into English was not very good but studied in parallel with the original French we managed to decipher that this 'event' may centre around the appearance and dangers of bulls. We had no idea at the time but were soon to learn, we had arrived in the middle of the bull fight season and on further exploration sure enough we discovered the bull ring, a small but perfectly formed arena, with seating all around.

The following day, just after a lazy *al fresco* lunch on *Starry Vere's* poop deck, we were alerted by a Spanish style fanfare of trumpets, being relayed around the village by a loud-speaker system fixed to each available lamppost and tree. The fanfare had that Bull fight character so off we set to see what was afoot. Not far from our boats, in a car park area at the canal end of the main street, we came across a flurry of activity. A small group of horsemen sporting all the wild-west gear and perched on excited white horses circled round a small cattle truck, the contents of which were about to be unloaded. Down dropped the tailgate of the truck releasing half a dozen very frisky, well horned, black bulls. The fanfare had certainly been a call to begin the festivities but not, as we would expect in the safe confines of the arena, no, it was about to happen right here, in a very public main street. There were no barriers or fences; all was left to the skills of the horsemen who with whistles and shouts steered the whole ensemble off at a gallop up the street toward the centre of the village and the adoring cheering crowds. A test of horsemanship maybe, but bulls and horses galloping down the street? Not an everyday occurrence where we come from.

Now, what we hadn't grasped was that horsemen and bulls turn round and gallop back and yes, we had started to walk down a suspiciously deserted street, hoping to find the action. The action found us! Bulls and cowboys heading back down the street in a cloud of dust, amid a chorus of whooping and cheering, straight toward us. We had a hasty choice to make, either shelter behind a rather pathetic tree or jump over someone's garden hedge. We made do with the tree. Amazingly this spectacle really seemed designed just for local amusement for, along with our new found New Zealand friends, we were the only tourists around and despite the crazy happenings around us we felt quite privileged to be there.

So, with initial warm up completed, the business then moved to the arena but not before an aperitif or two from the temporary wayside bar erected on the road outside the café. It was now the turn of young, white clad, Toreadors from a school for Toreadors in Arles, to show off their skills and do battle with the bulls. The traditional Spanish bullfight, with its ritual killing, does not appeal to us in any way but the Camargue version is very different and the bull definitely survives to see another day. Thankfully there were no weapons, no swords or spears, not even a red cloak. It was all really quite innocent, with just a show of bravado and nerve as the Toreadors attempted to seize a rosette fastened onto the head of each animal. A succession of bulls had their moment in the ring, I suspect they are the stars rather than the brave young men. They, that is the bulls, are especially bred for their task - perhaps the young men are as well - a stocky black Camargue variety, not particularly large but sporting serious looking horns capable of inflicting injury. The bullring at Gallician is modest in size and it was a little worrying when a beast jumped from the arena, over the wall and into the seating area. This happened on a number of occasions, the audience got very excited, they loved it but we prudently sat further back from the action, with an escape route planned.

All very exciting but the best was yet to come in the grand finale, the *bandido*, a staged 'escape' of the bulls, where they are released to run through the streets, which in Gallician means a direct route down to the canal towpath. The good news? Well, by the time this happens the bulls are so shattered their only desire is to find the nearest bit of pasture for a rest and a munch.

Into the evening the frontier town image grew ever more vivid with the erection of a roadside casino, complete with roulette wheel. As darkness fell the party began in earnest. Live country music twanged and whined, dancing spread down the street and a free flowing open-air bar kept everyone happy. Without doubt the aim was to have a good time but the atmosphere of the community impressed us. It was definitely a family event and with no apparent abuse of drink the evening continued in good humour with the police, as had been the case all day, noticeable by their absence.

The only thing that worried us... the odd stray bull!

13

...a castrated cockerel

It was almost November. One further day on the canal and our cruising would be over for the year. We had five months booked in Port Ariane to look forward to, certainly time to explore how we felt about living in France but the journey was not complete. We had reached the south and as we cruised along the canal in very agreeable Autumn sunshine the sea beckoned, a tantalising flash of light at times visible between sand dunes, or across the main coastal road in-between the sea-side buildings but it would have to wait until next year.

We had no idea what to expect of Lattes, or its marina, Port Ariane. On our map it appeared to be a very small place sitting on the River Lez, midway between the city of Montpellier and the seaside resort of Palavas les Flottes. My immediate thought was of a picturesque small village complete with traditional stone quay, hopefully full of character and a dash of old world charm perhaps. Nothing could have been further from the reality for after leaving the canal at Palavas and taking a right into the river we were into a quite different experience. The suddenly narrow navigable channel twisted and turned between great swathes of bamboo growing on each bank. We met just one lock to negotiate, then under a road bridge, a turn to starboard, through a large gated entrance and suddenly we were transported into a world that at first we knew not what, but my romantic vision was way off the mark.

The port was obviously new and certainly modern. High-rise apartment blocks on all four sides painted in warm yellows, oranges and ochre with architectural features we were later to realise taking inspiration from France's North African links; spiral staircases, decorative arches and fluted columns. It was all a little bemusing, not at all what we were expecting but our welcome was friendly with Andy and Barbara already settled in and there to greet our arrival. It seemed rather like moving into a new house on a modern housing estate, with the neighbours ready to meet us.

"Finished with engines", advised an English voice as I reversed *Starry Vere* into our spot. The friendly voice belonged to Stuart, one of the first to take our ropes and with a cheery bearded smile he asked where we were from in the UK.

"Nottingham", I remembered.

"Oh, my wife Jackie was born in Nottingham".

"Really, what a small world".

"Yes, in fact she's going back next week to see her niece. To a small village called Calverton".

"No... you'd never believe it but I was brought up in Calverton. My mother still lives there".

"Yes. Jackie is stopping in an old people's place, her niece is the warden".

"No!"

"Yes. I think it's called Nabarro Court".

"No..!! Stuart, do you know what our surname is?"

The first person we met and such a staggering coincidence. As it happens the sheltered accommodation in Calverton was named after my father, a prominent local politician in his day.

No sooner had we been introduced to Jackie then along came Keith, dog under arm.

"Hello, pleased to meet you. I'm Keith, my wife is Jennie, we're on the barge Gulliver"

Moored opposite us, on the opposite side of the street so to speak, a very smart, modern, yet traditional style barge.

"Did I hear you say Nottingham"

"Yes…"

"Jennie and I are from Nottingham"

"No!"

"Yes. Lambley to be precise"

"Never!"

Lambley, a small village not three miles from our house in Nottingham, a village I have known all my life. What a way to feel immediately at home, it was a promising start.

We set about discovering the place that would be our home for the next five months. Port Ariane had been built some five years before, a centrepiece in what was obviously an ambitious and very rapid expansion plan. Building was happening at a pace, block after block of apartments, attractive estates of individual villas and all the necessary commerce one would expect to service the needs of a community with spending power. There was evidence of the very small hamlet Lattes had probably been twenty years or more before but the tiny ancient church and smattering of old stone buildings had long since been submerged by modern development. The whole place was certainly upwardly mobile, quite probably a dormitory for the nearby and equally upwardly mobile city of Montpellier.

Lattes also had an interesting ancient history as a major Roman settlement and a fine museum bares witness to the many archaeological finds and artefacts. It's also but a stone's throw from wonderful Camargue terrain; the beautiful salt-water lakes, or *etangs* as they are known, are just a five-minute cycle ride out toward the sea and home to a spectacular flock of picture post card pink flamingos. The area is a protected nature reserve teaming with Camargue wild life. Cycling around the etangs we often came face to face with a herd of white horses, quite wild and often mischievous; they had learnt that a bag or a rucksack could contain someone's lunch. Herons and White Eagrets patrolled the water's edge with an abundance of many smaller species of bird life in the bushes and trees. We were privileged to spot a nesting pair of Storks high on a purpose built pole and all so vivid in the brilliant light. A cycle ride alongside the river, skirting round the etangs and ending up at the sea became one of our favourite and regular excursions.

So, it appeared we were in a place with one foot in the past, another stepping out into the future, brilliant local countryside close by, a short ride to the sea and an equally short cycle ride into Montpellier. This should make life very interesting.

Back in the port we became acquainted with our pontoon neighbours. There were twenty boats moored on the pontoon and a goodly number of owners would be living aboard for at least part of the winter. We were a cosmopolitan bunch to begin with. The Brits seemed to have the edge on numbers but there were four Dutch vessels, a New Zealander, Australian, German, Anglo American, and two or three French. Only the Brits and the Dutch remained for the winter duration and although all was genial and friendly two separate social groups became established along national lines.

Interestingly it was the first year away from Britain for all of the British boats so together we were discovering, experiencing and formulating for the first time. It was probably a blessing that no one couple amongst us had previous experience and that extra knowledge to impart. The group narrowed down as some left to return to the UK for the winter (I could never quite understand this, the winter seems the best time *not* to be in Britain) and we became five couples for the main duration. Andy and Barbara in *Saxton Chieftain*, a young couple, well, certainly younger than the rest of us, and hailing from Devon. Paul and Fearn in the catamaran *Force Five*. Paul was definitely from northern England but they had left Britain from the south coast. Roger and Sylvia, in *Phylella*, also from Devon, and Keith and Jennie, as we discovered also from Nottingham in *Gulliver*. Lots in common of course but living in close proximity the differences do begin to show, particularly during the many impromptu social events, when a few bottles of wine have been dealt with. Still, we made it to Christmas and enjoyed our first Christmas party afloat and all together but soon after the little community did start to unravel. It was inevitable. Initially we had all been thrown together in new surroundings but gradually we looked outwards, forging friendships with other boat owners in the port and eventually amongst the locals.

The nearby bar l'Aquarelle became our focal point. We had watched developments with interest as one of the many empty commercial properties around the port was transformed and with neither fuss nor fanfare it opened for business. It was certainly out of season, passing trade was a little thin and we were not sure whether it was an act of faith or folly on the part of the proprietor, although we thought it our duty to provide our brave friend with his first customers. The bar remained somewhat quiet most of the time but to the delight of the patron and his wife we began using it as a communal meeting place for a regular Sunday afternoon rendezvous. Marvellous co-operation from Sylvian in the local tourist office helped publicise our existence with an invitation for local people to join us. A lively weekly gathering was established where anyone who spoke English or wanted to, or, conversely, anyone who spoke French or wanted to, came together for an informal chat. These sessions even made the local paper, the *Midi Libre*. One headline blazed out, 'LA ARMADA EST ARRIVÉE', but we were under no illusion, the impending local mayoral elections probably had more to do with this attention than an attempt at *entente cordial*. We took it all in good spirit and indeed worked it to our advantage. Since its evident controversial construction the port had become a 'white cabbage' as the French say and the politicians were keen to show that it was now flourishing. Predictably, once the election was won or lost, it all went very quiet. No matter, we enjoyed the socialising enormously and established many new friendships. Janet and I certainly met some very interesting people and our stay in Lattes was made more memorable for it.

First there was Jacqueline, with her friends Guy and Madeline. Jacqueline lives in nearby Montpellier, in retirement from her profession of paediatrician. She is an imposing character, generous in every way. Obviously

116

well travelled she speaks some English but as Janet and I struggled with our French, Jacqueline, always keen that we should get it right, doggedly refused to let us off the hook until a nuance of pronunciation was perfect. At times she was quite formidable but great fun. Guy and Madeline had retired to Lattes, as had quite a number of people we met. Guy was a scientist but one with a well developed sense of humour. Madeline had a social conscience and concerned herself with many environmental and social issues. She had very good English but only helped when we were struggling in French to the point of collapse. All in all we enjoyed the company of this trio and were particularly flattered when Jacqueline invited us to join her for dinner on Christmas Eve. We knew the French place much store on the Christmas Eve meal so we were looking forward to it and as Ben was arriving to spend Christmas with us he was invited too.

There was certainly no hint of a white Christmas this far south, although it was pouring with rain when Guy and Madeline transported us to Jacqueline's chic Montpellier apartment. It was a good size gathering and we were introduced to her friends and her sister, as the first bottle of champagne was festively uncorked. Our host was obviously toiling in the kitchen so we did our best at small talk before being ushered to the large table.

Jacqueline was relishing her role as hostess and with some ceremony a first course of smoked salmon arrived; a lovely piece of fish but accompanied with nothing more than a generous top-up of our champagne flutes. On to a second course and another set of plates arrive, each precariously balancing a lonely, large, pure white, Boudon sausage. Nothing else, just this very large albino sausage. Oh, and more champagne. My challenge now was not to catch the eye of Janet or Ben, we may have disgraced ourselves! Then the main course, it was to be chicken but it appeared, not ordinary chicken and this presented an opportunity to have some fun with the visitors. With great delight the assembled gathering set about a game of culinary charades; explaining… no… demonstrating, in a wild mixture of French and expressive sign language, the very nature of this bird and what had befallen it. With increasing hilarity all became clear, it was what we call a capon… a castrated cockerel! Cause for another top up of champagne all round as servings of this unfortunate beast arrived, garnished with a few token mushrooms and the cooking juices from the pan. As everyone started eating it was clear there was to be no accompaniment, not a veggie in sight, just an endless supply of champagne. Cheese followed, just cheese, and to finish, a token non-animal product, the Christmas Yule log… with even more champagne. We had eaten well and drunk to excess; we had been entertained and been the subject of entertainment but the only green we had seen all night was the Christmas tree! Later in the New Year we invited Jacqueline, Guy and Madeline to eat with us on *Starry Vere* …and vegetables were served.

As so often happens Ben left as Emma and Adam arrived for a New Year break. We enjoyed a festive dinner in the company of Jennie and Keith with whom we had got into the habit of sharing many a meal. We realised our tastes in wine, food, music, sense of humour, as well as the boaty things, gave us much in common. As midnight approached we all spilled out onto the pontoon and with the hour chiming the celebrations were supplemented by me playing Auld Lang Syne on the trumpet. Not sure how that happened but it was painful.

The weather began to really improve over the New Year and borrowing a couple of extra bikes from the hire boat company based in the port, we four cycled down to the beach at Palavas to enjoy a picnic in the sun, complete with driftwood barbecue. I almost felt sorry for Emma and Adam, returning to a real winter.

The festive season past, visitors safely returned, we settled down to our routine. People often ask, indeed in IT speak our most FAQ is, "what do you do all day?" Well, firstly we make it very clear that our life is not just a succession of lazy days in the sun. Oh no, it's a tough life. But seriously, we are always busy and there is certainly plenty to keep us occupied. The boat, for instance, is in need of constant attention. Although we began renovating *Starry Vere* shortly after we purchased five years earlier, the project goes on and on. I honestly think it will never be finished. Living on board we are always dreaming up improvements, sometimes cosmetic but mostly updating and refining systems and engineering. This is apart from the necessary regular painting and decorating, for although we like the sun our varnished wooden topsides don't. We have to freshen up the finish at least once a year, sometimes twice. It's very much a 'Forth Bridge' type exercise.

Until you've lived aboard with a bicycle as your main mode of transport, it's difficult to perceive what a big deal shopping can be. Out goes the concept of a big weekly shop, with burgeoning supermarket trolley emptied straight into the boot of a car. For us it's a case of little and often and usually at some distance but we enjoy the opportunity to blend into the local scene, plus it keeps us fit. We certainly don't feel deprived by the lack of four wheels, in fact we feel quite liberated! After dealing with the essentials of life we may then do a little sightseeing, read a book or two and squeeze in a modicum of socialising. Yes, it _is_ a tough life.

A knock on the side of the boat one afternoon and we are confronted by a rather smart gentleman trying to attract our attention. We open with a *'bonjour monsieur'* but it soon becomes clear that our caller speaks splendid English as he fluently explains that Sylvian in the tourist office has sent him our way. We are intrigued and naturally do the honourable thing by inviting him on board for a cup of tea. As an Anglophile our guest probably appreciated this gesture more than we imagined. Bernard was his name and General was his rank; we had a guest from the French military, retired to be precise but he was calling on military business. It transpired that the General, as we subsequently always referred to him, had a modest mission to ensure the French army spoke English. He was very candid about his own career, insisting that an important factor in his rise from the ranks to General was his talent and passion for languages. The French army, like much of French society, has regarded most things not French as being on the periphery of importance. There was little inclination or perceived need to speak English, even when working alongside British, American or most other foreign forces, who do insist on a working knowledge of English. A couple of weeks later we were fortunate to meet a number of senior officers from other nations, working as military attachés in Montpellier. We learnt that in the not so distant past, particularly during the troubles in former Yugoslavia, there was much frustration among the multi-national force because French senior personnel insisted on working only in French. Allegedly, many important decisions were delayed whilst documents were laboriously translated. On a more positive note it appears that this situation has now been reversed with the modern French military demanding all senior personnel and certainly any aspiring officers to have a command of English.

The General had tracked us down with a purpose. He was organising a language dinner on behalf of his students and we were to be invited with the proviso that we speak English. We could manage that. English speaking ex-military were what he was really looking for but there we had to disappoint, my stint in the boy scouts was the nearest I got to a uniform and Janet didn't even make the Girl Guides. We might be able to help though. Moored over on the other side of the port was the classic Dutch barge *Beatrix*, with owners Al and Julie in residence. We had only met a couple of times, they were obviously American but I had heard that Al was no less than a retired American Navy Captain. He should fit the bill perfectly and surely a Captain would be a fine enough catch to compensate for my lowly rank of Baden Powell *patrol second*. The General departed, content with his conscripts and we awaited further orders.

Although we now spend a great deal of our time around sea level, in our pre-boating days leisure time was often spent walking in the hills and minor mountains of Britain. Annual holidays usually meant indulging our Francophile tendencies and for ten consecutive years we aimed for the same idyllic spot, high in the Pyrenees, right on the border with Spain. Longstanding friends of ours from Nottingham, Pete and Elspeth, with their son Patrick, arranged to visit us for a week in February. They are also keen on the fresh air life, Pete has trekked the length of the Pyrenees at least twice and so it was likely that an opportunity to clamber off into the quite striking and rugged area north of Montpellier would not be missed.

Sure enough they arrived equipped with hire car and we spent a few happy days exploring. The Pic St.Loup was conquered, a spectacular rock that rises dramatically from a flat plain, famous for wine bearing the same name. Once up on the peak there is a tremendous three hundred and sixty degree vista and the opportunity to come face to face with glider pilots who seem to enjoy zooming around the sheer faces of the rock. Then, further west, to the rocky gorges around the River Herault's dramatic tumble to the sea, the village of St.Guilhem le Desert and the challenge of the surrounding hills. The weather was absolutely brilliant and even at these albeit modest altitudes (by Pete's standards) we were down to shirtsleeves. With a beautifully clear sky offering incredible views it proved to be a very pleasant change for all of us and an opportunity to dig out the hiking boots we had stowed away, just in case our 'mountain goat' friend came to stay.

The General reported back and one February evening, along with Americans Al and Julie, we negotiated our way into the local Army base, guests, but with an important mission. The evening was informal in that uniforms were not worn but our welcome from the student officers and their superiors was warm although a little stiff. We soon appreciated it was a little tricky for the students. They were obviously unaccustomed and initially uncomfortable socialising with their senior officers and this apart from conversing with native English speakers, whether the genuine article or the American version. Ouch! A drink or two relaxed the evening and over dinner we did what was requested of us and talked.

We also learnt.

Our perception of 'students' had to be quickly revised for the youngish new recruits turned out to be highly qualified professionals and on our table alone we had the pleasure of meeting four young lawyers. The Army had actively been recruiting quality entrants to serve its modern needs; we found it very illuminating and realised what a stereotyped vision we held of the military.

A young lady, Dominique, sat next to me and proved to be linguistically very competent and certainly keen to improve. Although a qualified lawyer and with a husband and two young children, she had made this career decision which meant living some distance away from her home town, at least for the initial year of training. She was a lovely person and Janet and I felt quite honoured when later that week the General relayed an invitation to us to attend what I suppose we would call a passing out parade, followed by a celebratory lunch; this is the French army of course. For Dominique it was a very important event in her Army career and she had invited us as her guests.

The parade took place in the most beautiful historic courtyard under a perfectly blue crisp Mediterranean winter sky. The General graciously took the role of guide and we were treated to a tour round the buildings. He quite obviously lived for the Army, it was certainly his whole life and he was proud of its traditions, reminiscing about the time as a new recruit he had been part of the same ceremony. The format probably hasn't changed in centuries and involves each new recruit receiving their sword, a symbol of their induction. This simple act forms part of a pageant demonstrating military pomp alongside sheer theatrical artistry. The uniforms were stunning. We tend to think of the British Army as second to none when it comes to drill and precision but what we experienced was very impressive. It was quite moving to be present at a ceremony even few French citizens will have witnessed. The magic moment though and one that I will always treasure, was the singing of the French national anthem, the Marseilles. For me this great republican outburst is the tops, a really successful national anthem but when a parade-ground of soldiers begin to sing this great song with apparent spontaneity, an abundance of passion and a stirring commitment, the effect was powerful and mesmerising. Yes, I know it was planned with military precision but non-the-less it appeared absolutely spontaneous and the result was operatic in its theatre. I'll never forget it.

After the main ceremony the band led the parade for a march past, we were introduced to the current general, the commandant, who was charming as one would expect and then off to lunch, which stretched well into the afternoon. What a unique experience to reflect on and to ponder, *how on earth did we get there?*

The year was also marching on and for some time Janet and I had been debating the fate of our upstairs apartment back home in Nottingham; still ours but sitting empty for most of the time. Even an empty property costs money to maintain and quite simply it could be earning money for us. It meant severing a link, losing a refuge but once we got our head around the notion of not having a base in Britain we agreed on the decision to return and empty it, with a view to letting. We had reservations naturally but it helped when the apartment got a taker before we had even moved out. Fate seemed to be pushing us in a certain direction and despite the heartache it was a good move.

And so our five months in Lattes had passed. Very swiftly, probably because our lives were so full and busy. With satisfaction and pleasure, how could it be otherwise? Now we had nothing but enthusiasm for a new season of cruising. There were no second thoughts, no regrets. So far, so *very* good.

14

...salty anecdotes began to flow

For most of the time the bar l'Aquarelle seemed a dormant kind of establishment but as we approached on this particular Friday evening, the last in March, it was a pleasant surprise to find a large clientele spilling out onto the terrace. The sound of spoken English predominated and as we mingled it was clear the enthusiastic hubbub was boat talk. The kick-start to our new cruising season had begun. Over fifty enthusiastic members of the Dutch Barge Association had descended on Lattes for a visitor weekend, organised by port residents Michael and Rose of the narrow boat *Cloudcatcher*. With consummate skill Michael had enlisted the participation of half a dozen resident boats to give the visitors a canal cruise. We hadn't taken much persuading, after five months in Lattes we were keen to be off and this seemed an excellent, almost celebratory way of breaking out!

The following morning we woke surprisingly early to the sound of Paul's characteristic footsteps marching up the pontoon. This was unusual if not unique, as Paul and

Fearne, pontoon D's resident yachties in their catamaran *Force Five,* had gained a reputation for not being early risers. Paul had generously 'volunteered' to assist our early departure and as engines fired up and lines were cleared we headed in orderly pre-arranged fashion for lock number three, *troisieme ecluse,* which strange to say is the only lock on the river.

The flotilla of boats leaving Port Ariane represented a community that had gelled over the previous five months and although we all felt elated to be back on the water, there was sadness and even unease that the security, relationships and shared experiences had come to an end. This goes with the territory of course and subsequent winters will always see new boating communities rise and fall in any number of ports and marinas. It is fascinating how a disparate group of people are thrown together, bound only by the live-a-board life. Village life had always seemed attractive to us but having only lived in a city suburb this was possibly as close as we would get to the hothouse atmosphere of a small community.

So our flotilla wound its way down the River Lez in inspiring spring sunshine toward the Mediterranean port of Palavas les Flots. Access to the sea at Palavas is restricted by a very low bridge but our mooring for the weekend was to be the port de plaisance, just past the junction with the canal du Rhône a Sete, in readiness for the embarkation of our guests the following morning.

Sunday morning, April 1st brings one of those perfect mornings, it just could not be better. Our visiting crews are expected by 0830 so another early start; we suspect Paul, who is not taking part in the trip, is still tucked up in *Force 5* recovering from the shock of the previous morning. Our guests for the day arrive promptly, introductions are made and we are soon underway cruising east along the canal, heading for the historic fortified city of Aigues Mort, retracing our route taken the previous autumn. The significance of the date had not been lost on some members of the group and word soon reaches us of a fine April fool joke devised by the crew of another flotilla member, *Flora Post*. Skipper/doctor Andrew with first-mate/nurse Patsy have, with understandable authority, warned their visitor crew of the prevalence of West Nile Fever in this area. Evidently the famous Carmague white horses suffer from it but by rubbing a light coating of cooking oil into the skin, protection is at hand. A supply of oil was generously provided but it appears the jest was spotted in time to prevent any embarrassment. A great way to break the ice though! The crew onboard *Starry Vere* chose an alternative ice breaker and with the skipper's approval cracked open a bottle of bubbly to celebrate being in a wonderful environment on such a splendid day.

The flotilla arrived regally in Aigues Mort by lunchtime and with excellent planning rafted alongside resident boats and barges in the port. *Starry Vere* moored alongside the thirty metre Dutch barge *Hoot* and British owners Dawn and David kindly invited us onto their sun terrace where the party atmosphere flourished with a very French lunch. For the return to Palavas a new crew joined ship and as with the outward group, we were pleased to play host to another set of friendly people who were keen to quiz us about every aspect of living aboard in France. The task of helming *Starry Vere* passed round the crew as we polished off the remaining food and drink provided for the trip. Salty anecdotes began to flow and a more relaxed group of people we suspect would never be found. Our arrival back at Palavas was in delightful early evening sun and our guests reluctantly disembarked to prepare for the evening meal in the restaurant Le Phare, a high-rise revolving affair that dominates the Palavas skyline. Although it has a sixties feel architecturally, it was built relatively recently and offers a superb 360-degree view of the area, land and sea. During dinner we were treated to the most spectacular sun set with vivid, ever changing reds colouring the waters of the etang, river and sea. A backdrop created by the range of hills north of Montpellier, including the Pic St. Loup, completed a scene to savour. The most beautiful end to a perfect day and a brilliantly planned weekend... if only the meal had been as good!

Monday morning was one of mixed emotion. With DBA visitors due to fly home we really did have to go our separate ways, yet we lingered. Our visitors wandered up and down the moorings; chatting, reminiscing, thanking, obviously very reluctant to head back to reality and even work. But we had a plan and in company with Keith and Jennie on *Gulliver*, not forgetting the dog Billie, we had decided to head back to Gallician to meet up with other Port Ariane residents, Roger and Sylvia on *Phylella*. My imminent birthday gave us an excuse for a party, although we reached such an acute state of relaxation the party was held on the wrong day. We made return visits to the small independent wine cave, *'Mas du Notair'*, and the excellent cave co-operative almost next door, to refresh cellars. In all we spent five happy days in Gallician enjoying perfect spring weather but finally we realised it was time to drag ourselves away from these delights and move on to new territory.

Over the winter months plans for the new season had been made and changed a number of times. Our intention had been to enter the sea and voyage down to Spain but this was eventually put on hold. In company with newfound friends we decided to take the opportunity of cruising the three linked waterways that connect the Mediterranean to the Atlantic. *La canal du midi, la canal lateral* and finally *la Gironde* that would take us on a giant sweep through the heartland of France.

We made our way back along the canal du Rhône a Sete for the final time. *Gulliver* had left before us; we were in company with *Phylella*. Once past the junction with the River Lez at Palavas we were into new territory. A night was spent moored in sight of the *abbey la Maguelone,* an impressive collection of stone buildings looking from afar as though an inland island amongst the sand and etangs. An island it indeed was but for many years it has been joined to the 'mainland' by a sand-spit that doubles as the main drive to accommodate the infernal motorcar. Its history is supposed to stretch back to the second century but today the main interest lies in the Romanesque cathedral, restored in the nineteenth century. We visited a couple of times during the winter by cycle and noticed that work was underway renovating and replacing a number of windows with modern stain glass designs. It is good to think that the place goes on developing with tasteful and respectful additions reflecting the early twenty-first century. It is also relevant to the present day in that the sea of vineyards surrounding the abbey are managed by an organisation, perhaps a charity, that provides employment for people with learning difficulties. So this ancient site, rather than remaining just a museum, has found a purpose for the present. The abbey is also home to a music festival each June and a truly wonderful setting it must be.

A very early start the following morning was necessary to catch the opening of the railway swing bridge at

Frontignan but the wind was beginning to blow, which is bad news in this flat exposed coastal landscape. If we were to be marooned by the Mistral, the unfriendly wind that howls down the Rhône valley and can blow for a week, then better off in Frontignan than the wilds of Maguelone. Nine o'clock is the official opening time of the bridge and it was a minute or two after as we came tearing up the canal but we made it and moored on the old attractive stone quay. *Gulliver* had arrived the previous day.

The small town of Frontignan is strategically situated just before the canal ends at the Etang du Thau, although in our humble opinion its significance is due more to wine than geographical positioning. It is famous for a sweet Muscat "pudding wine", as we know it aboard *Starry Vere*, with some locally produced examples unsurpassed for their honeyed quality. Our prize discovery though was not the sweet stuff but a Muscat Sec, produced by the local co-operative; fresher, lighter and beautifully fragrant. A number of bottles found their way into our 'cellar' with one miraculously surviving to the following Christmas in Spain. It was beautiful with Christmas pudding.

As all the handbooks say the Mistral can blow for a week and it certainly did. The effect on the nearby Etang de Thau, the large saltwater lake, was highly dramatic. Being connected directly to the Mediterranean the Mistral drives the water out into the sea and in the process creates a dramatic beam swell that would not be out of place in the open ocean. Crossing the Etang is the only route to reach the mouth of the canal du Midi, a voyage (for it is an inland sea) of some seventeen kilometres. We waited patiently in Frontignan, not too great a hardship with the distraction of wine tasting but eventually we took what appeared to be a lull as our cue to make the passage. A lull there may have been but once out of the lee of the land the feeling really was of being in mid-ocean as enormous broadside rollers attacked the boat and deposited vast quantities of salt over us. There was one consolation, the opportunity to open up *Starry Vere's* engines and blow away the effects of a year navigating on inland waterways. We were still cruising in company with *Phylella* and *Gulliver* but wisely Keith and Jennie in *Gulliver* decided to turn back; their wide beamed inland waterways barge was not designed for ocean passages! Sadly, a beautiful display of Geraniums taking pride of place on *Gulliver's* coach roof suffered terminally from a salt drenching.

As always there are conflicting reports to every experience. On relating our harrowing tale to Paul and Fearne, who had crossed the Etang a week or so earlier in *Force Five,* their experience was of a glass like surface, visibility to the bottom and stopping for a swim half way across! Swimming may have been out of the question for us but we could have certainly got off and walked. As we entered the mouth of the canal du Midi we virtually came to a halt with *Starry Vere* ploughing a furrow along the bottom. It was not until we reached the first lock, the ecluse du Bagnas, that some semblance of depth was reinstated. We didn't realise how prophetic it was of things to come.

15

...and you Madam, you are an absolute dragon!

The canal du Midi is a remarkable example of seventeenth century industrial engineering, conceived and built by Pierre Paul Riquet between 1663 and 1681. It leaves the southern tip of the Etang de Thau, almost within sight of the Mediterranean, to weave a delicious route inland through southwest France, linking the important towns of Agde, Beziers, Carcassonne and Castelnaudary, before reaching the major city of Toulouse. Initially constructed as a commercial waterway the canal is now a designated world heritage site with a use purely for pleasure and as a consequence one of the most popular cruising waterways in France. For me it is the natural beauty that impresses most. The perpetual welcome shade offered by enormous one hundred year old Plane trees lining the canal, their enormous towering trunks a subtle mosaic of greys, greens and yellows. Looking over to the south, far in the distance, the snow-capped Pyrenees form a dramatic backdrop to complement a foreground of tantalising wall-to-wall vineyards; precise, corduroy like, elgantly manicured, row after row.

There is a price to pay for navigating what is after all a living museum, one set in stunning scenery with such a conducive climate and that cost is a surfeit of hire boats, or 'bumper boats' as we affectionately call them. To be fair the notoriety enjoyed by hire-boaters, which has reached folklore status amongst the boat owning fraternity, is not due to the actions of all holidaymakers...*just the majority!* Quite large boats are available for hire *'sans permis'*, with inveriably inexperienced crews taking charge, determined to drive and park their vessels like the cars they have left behind. The canal has reached saturation point but of course the health of the local economy and indeed the very survival of the canal are at stake. We had been advised to be through and up beyond Toulouse before the busiest holiday period of July and August.

But it was still only April; we felt no need to rush and anyway the canal was quite beautiful in its first flush of spring. Along each bank prolific beds of Iris-like flowers edging the water with a brilliant yellow and arcs of massive Plane trees sporting their first fresh light-green canopy. We lingered in the ancient city of Agde, one of the oldest towns in France with many of its ancient buildings constructed from the austere black basilic lava gathered from the nearby Pic St Loup and met up with friends Ted and Sue whom we had initially met back on the River Trent in Britain. Our progress was relaxed and uneventful until the approach to Beziers, where an encounter with a 'bumper boat' gave us a nasty moment.

The canal is shallow for *Starry Vere* at the best of times and we need to hold a centre course for the deeper water. This particular 'bumper boat' was heading down the canal toward us on a collision course and seemingly oblivious to our presence. Foolishly, never to be repeated, I moved over to starboard to accommodate them and... bang, we hit a car! Yes, a car, a green car. Be assured I was sober and the car was not on dry land but submerged below the water. With an alarming jolt our stern lifted clean out of the water as the starboard propeller made contact. Bearing in mind *Starry Vere* weighs in fully laden (as we certainly are) at around twenty tons, it was an unnerving moment and with damage immediately indicated by heavy vibration transmitting through the helm. Struggling to pull back the throttles and keep the boat under control I was vaguely aware of the 'bumper boat' cruising by, its crew brandishing wine glasses and oblivious to our plight. I was even too pre-occupied to curse them!

Having twin engines prevented us from being stranded and initially we thought it best to limp on using just the port engine and catch up with *Phylella* in Beziers. Once safely moored we needed to consider our best course of action. My hope was that we could continue up the canal using mainly one engine and haul the boat out for repairs at the end of the season, prior to heading out to sea. But after another dose of severe vibration, as we attempted to move on, it was clear the damage was serious; we needed to investigate without delay. Our best course of action was to limp back to Agde, where it is possible to lock down onto the River Herault and seek help at the highly recommended Allemandes boatyard, situated very close to the river's entry into the sea at Grau D'Agde. Oh, how did we know it was a green car? As we were later to discover, the propeller blade that made contact had a large swathe of green paint on it. We have since heard that the police and canal authorities retrieve up to two hundred cars a year, dumped in the canal as a result of theft, vandalism and even suicide attempts.

Happily, what started as a distressing incident gave way to quite an enjoyable if not expensive experience. Allemandes boatyard is a family run business, primarily serving the local fishing industry and yachting fraternity. It also boasts one of the best chandlery stores I have seen, an Aladdin's cave of a place. Founders of the business, Monsieur et Madame Allemande senior, are still very much involved but the boat yard part of the business now revolves around their son Henri Allemande, a brilliant but eccentric engineer.

As *Starry Vere* was lifted out our problem became immediately obvious, the starboard propeller was not hanging at the same angle as the port. Amazingly it was not the propeller that was bent but the shaft, directly behind the prop, which is extraordinary for a one and three-quarter-inch diameter stainless steel shaft. No problem for our brilliant engineer (the extent of his 'English' being *"no probleme"*) and the shaft, once removed, was whisked away to the very extensive workshops. We then waited... and waited... took the opportunity to undertake a little *painting and decorating* and watched the world go by on the river, directly in front of us. We soon realised it was no good expecting a deadline at Allemandes. Henri is a law unto himself; all passes at his relaxed pace and for a couple of days we just carried on waiting.

We did learn though, apart from repairing and building boats, the family also dabble in aeroplanes – home made aeroplanes. One lovely evening Henri pulled out of the workshops a small, single prop, two-seater seaplane, on the face of it quite unsophisticated. Still in his blue overhauls, long dark hair reaching his shoulders, the picture of a seventies French film star complete with cigarette hanging from lip, he pushed the plane down the slipway into the river and jumped onboard. Once midstream the engine barked into life and the plane, still firmly afloat, set off down the river toward the sea. We followed along the bank, camera at the ready, as gradually the plane accelerated but still it remained waterborne. What a visiting boat cruising up the river from the sea would have made of it I dread to think - the locals probably take it in their stride. Then, as the plane left the river and entered the open sea, it lifted up into a perfectly blue evening sky and disappeared buzzing down the coast for a couple of hours. We speculated on a possible assignation, a very romantic image, rather like the Milk Tray adverts. Later, during our forced but enjoyable stay at Allemandes, we were able to visit the workshops and noticed a mark two, bigger and better seaplane under construction. Amazing!

Eventually, with propeller shaft skilfully straightened, musician turned engineer helped put it all back together again and we were whisked back into the water. Before Henri would release us from his charge he came on board to check all was well and climbing down into the engine room he was immediately fascinated by *Starry Vere's* unusual Rootes Lister engines. In halting French I tried to explain their unconventional design; two-stroke, supercharged, horizontally apposed pistons etc., just the kind of content included in the BBC language course. I wasn't getting very far so I resorted to digging out the engine handbooks to satisfy his excitement and interest. Mental note: if ever we have a serious engine problem or

Out on the hard at Allemandes, Henri's seaplane in the foreground.

particularly if a component needs to be manufactured, Allemandes is the place to be.

Janet and I decided we would not let this incident divert us from our original plan and so, if a little tentatively, we retraced our steps back up the canal to Beziers, to spend a week in the busy and interesting canal port. Beziers was the birthplace of Paul Riquet so we needed to pay due homage at the statue erected in his honour, situated, strange to say, a good walk from the canal in the centre of town. Beziers must have been an important transitional stage on the canal when the waterways were at their height of importance and as such a thriving commercial centre. As with so many canals it was the busy railway line, perversely in this case often running alongside the canal, that was responsible for their demise over a century ago. The area is now a magnet for both tourists and local visitors with two other examples of Riquet's remarkable vision and architectural legacy proving to be enduringly popular.

Continuing upstream out of the port, a very deep lock lifted *Starry Vere* onto a much higher level, and then almost immediately we were crossing *Le pont canal sur l'Orb*, the magnificent stone aqueduct built to transport the canal over the substantial width of the River Orb. It's an odd sensation, cruising in a boat *over* a river and with the view of the town and Bezier cathedral sitting on the high ground off the starboard side it is all quite spectacular.

A little further on and we reached the second equally impressive piece of canal engineering, the 'flight' or 'staircase' of locks at Foncerannes. Seven consecutive lock chambers lift or drop boats a total of almost fourteen metres. Its reputation is such that tourists, often by the busload, arrive to watch us boaters make the difficult ascent (it's much easier coming down). As each successive lock gate is opened, often by a not so sympathetic eclusier, the force of water tumbling down from lock to lock is formidable and rather like all spectator sports, they love to see things go wrong! These locks are a real test of teamwork, sometimes the test is failed and raised voices and the apportioning of blame are often in evidence.

Once the gauntlet has been run, and for those who know, there is a reward available in the form of a splendid and typical small vineyard. We moored at the top of the flight and led by the crew of *Gulliver*, who did know, walked for no more than five minutes away from the canal to find the *Domaine de Mi Côte*. It was one of those idyllic moments, a romantic TV moment that you think can't really happen. But it did for us and as we walked down the main drive, between the rows of vines, the proprietor-vigneron climbed down from his tractor and led us into the cave for a tasting. There is nothing better than chatting to the guy who made the wine. We staggered back to the boat with our booty, bought at a price that would be unfair to mention.

There is a further delight to enjoy after negotiating the Foncerannes locks; fifty-four kilometres of blissful lock-free cruising. Riquet, in a brilliant piece of surveying, managed to follow the natural contour of the land and create what surely must be one of the most relaxed and beautiful lengths of inland waterway anywhere. Charming and historic villages come and go and the very first canal tunnel, *Percee de Malpas*, is negotiated with wonder. There is an opportunity to visit a site of great historic and archaeological interest just a short walk from the canal, the *Oppidum d'Enserune*. Couple all this with anything like the magnificent weather we experienced and it is not surprising the canal is such a popular holiday destination. We were certainly glad not to have been deterred by our mishap and our persistence was to be rewarded by a wonderful and unique view of rural France.

Boat rage is alive and well on the canal du Midi! Still in company with Keith, Jennie and the dog Billy, on the their Yorkshire built barge, *Gulliver*, we had spent a couple of very pleasant days in the small community of Capestang. As normal we departed at a leisurely pace, navigated through one of the lowest and tightest arched bridges on the canal and looked forward to a relaxed morning cruise to our planned destination. Two hire boats had left about the same time and were coming up fast behind us. We cruise at about the legal limit so it shouldn't be necessary to move over to let boats pass, apart from the fact that the canal is narrow and the only 'deep' water is down the centre - our sejour in Grau D'Agde still fresh in the memory! The two hire boats drew closer and closer to our stern, adopting a definitely aggressive posture. Yes, boats do have body language and these were obviously intent on overtaking. The first boat began to draw alongside, squeezing in between the left bank and us. All we could do was hold our course (and curse) but coming up ahead was a sharp left-hand bend. *Starry Vere's* outside steering position is generally much higher than most hire boats and what my good friend helming the hire boat couldn't see, was another hire boat bearing down toward us, around the approaching bend. The overtaking hire boat kept on coming, pushing a bow wave with his excessive speed that was swamping the canal bank and he was directly alongside before he caught first glimpse of the potential disaster. Aided and abetted by his first mate back seat driver and with the first stages of panic setting in, he

The canal du Midi, lined with spectacular Plain trees.

oscillated frantically between speeding up and slowing down, at a complete and utter loss what to do. The hire boat bearing down on two craft filling the width of the canal resorted to the horn but for some unfathomable reason resisted the sensible option of slowing down. Finally, as the impasse was reached, I had no option but to slam on *Starry Vere's* brakes, which meant a very rapid burst of hard astern, allowing the over-taker to squeeze under our bow, back onto his rightful side of the canal. Hopefully his first mate gave him the earful he deserved but I suspect it was entirely our fault for not moving into the autobahn's slow lane.

But no lessons had been learnt. The overtaking hire boat, undaunted and unashamed, lined himself up ahead for a further manoeuvre to pass *Gulliver* while the second following boat, still closely astern and whose crew must have witnessed everything, decided they were not to be outdone. Relentlessly they also edged alongside, we on *Starry Vere* trying desperately to keep cool and with eyes rigidly facing forward they squeezed past. It was not until they were a safe distance ahead that they displayed their true colours; both skipper and first mate launched into a bizarre tirade of ridiculous aerobics, verbal abuse and sign language, 'enquiring' as to why we had not moved over. How could we begin to explain? How could we tell them we were still smarting from the cost of the last repair?

Luckily, for them, we had a planned rendezvous at Argeliers with friends Roger and Sylvia aboard '*Phylella*', so we stopped before we could meet up with the crazy hire boats again… for of course on the canal there is no hiding place. It was Roger's birthday and along with Jennie and Keith, not forgetting Billy, we enjoyed a bank-side birthday barbecue. Roger and Sylvia were on their way back down the canal, aiming for the ocean. They were unnerved by the lack of depth and keen to leave the canal before the possibility of a summer drought. We thought about it but decided to keep going, it was all so beautiful, an opportunity we may not get again.

The next few days of cruising immediately vindicated our decision and blessed by superb early summer weather we enjoyed delight after delight. After two days of gentle cruising beyond Argeliers, we came across a gem of a spot. Shaded by Plane trees, adjacent to a classic arched Midi bridge, magnificent view across agricultural land, vineyards and high hills in the distance, this simple bank-side mooring was all we could ask for. The nearest village was Puicheric, demanding the hardship of a two-kilometre walk for the bread down a country lane alive with bird life and bursting with wild spring flowers on both sides. This proved to be one of our all time favourite moorings with the bonus of absolute nocturnal silence and really dark darkness.

Conveniently we arrived in the city of Carcassonne on our thirtieth wedding anniversary. The approach by canal offers splendid views of the celebrated medieval city, a genuine yet Disney-like double walled city, complete with turrets and towers. Needless to say it is a massive tourist attraction and once inside those impressive double walls the reality is a plethora of tourist shops. We last visited it by car over ten year earlier and it is obvious the commercial pressure of tourism has taken its toll. Best viewed from a distance we think.

Over many centuries the city has spread out from the old walls and the central square of this 'new' city is a typically French wide-open space. The French have confidence to leave spaces uncluttered, resisting a British urge to fill them with 'useful' structures like wrought iron flower display holders. We make the comparison with our hometown of Nottingham, which has a potentially wonderful central space, the Old Market Square. On our last visit to the homeland we were disappointed that the square had become cluttered with what appeared to be the complete catalogue of pseudo Victorian street furniture, plus a bizarre selection of exotic flowerbeds surrounded by protective fencing. Nottingham's central square was conceived as a large open gathering space, indeed the traditional Goose Fair used to be held on this site. Perhaps these days an open space is seen as a threat?

The only congestion in the Carcassonne square was a surfeit of lunchtime diners enjoying the selection of characterful cafés and restaurants, each doing brisk trade in the mid-day sun of late May. Although Janet and I had been married for thirty years this particular year seemed special, almost a new beginning, deserving to be celebrated by joining the lunch-time atmosphere with a table in the sun and a plate of moules et frites, washed down with a bottle of chilled rosé.

For us the downside to Carcassonne is the canal port. It seemed very well organised and modern but so were the charges, making it probably the most expensive mooring on the canal. Crucially it is also completely without shade but by cruising on, just a little way out of the built up area, we soon found ourselves back under the canopy of plane trees and able to relax on another peaceful bank-side mooring, yet close enough to pop back to the town by boat or cycle for shopping and sight-seeing.

A couple of days cruising after leaving the activity of Carcassonne we came across what we can only describe as a living museum exhibit. Adjacent to the simple wooden mooring pontoon at Villepinte there is an example of a typical canal-side laundry area, provided far before the days of twin tubs and front loaders, even before the advent of electricity. This facility consists of a bank-side stone trough with a draining board type structure giving access to the water at a convenient arm height. Quite often these wash areas were fitted out with a roof and must have provided a popular spot for socialising whilst labouring over the week's washing. We assumed their useful life was long over but not in Villepinte. As we approached the mooring we noticed two very elderly ladies hard at work, washing clothes in the canal. With back's bent and scarves over heads they spent a whole afternoon soaping, beating (with a wooden spatula-like instrument) and copiously rinsing in the somewhat green waters of the canal, not a couple of metres from *Gulliver's* bow. The mooring is a good three kilometres from the actual community of Villepinte, the nearest village, so we wondered in amazement, why? Long established routines do live on out in this very rural region and these two ladies must have been following this particular routine for many, many years. But, we speculated, did they know what went into the canal these days? Eventually son or daughter arrived in a horseless carriage to transport the washing and washers home; they should seriously be considering a washing machine this Christmas! As we departed the following morning little did we realise this peaceful spot would be the scene for another of our 'triumphs', but more of that on the return leg!

The last major centre before the canal ends at Toulouse is the attractive town of Castelnaudary. The waterway opens out dramatically into *Le Grand Bassin*, a seven-hectare lake created to feed the staircase of four locks that have to be negotiated. Not as dramatic perhaps as the Foncerannes staircase in Beziers but bear in mind Castelnaudary is home to a major hire boat base. Every weekend, during the holiday season, boatloads of new holidaymakers cast off and if they decide to go east toward Carcassonne - and most do - their first experience of a lock is this staircase. True, locks are easier descending but a very small summit pound means manoeuvring space is very tight and in the summer, when there are a multitude of boats, we witnessed many a crazy race to enter the top lock first as the gates open. The competitive urge is still present and it's a pity they are not persuaded to go west first, at least for a couple of days, to get the hang of helming and crucially, adapt to a slower pace of life.

Castelnaudary is famous for Cassoulet. It claims to be the home of this dish, a wonderful stew of sausage, goose and beans. In our experience there are as many recipes as cooks in France but Castelnaudary Cassoulet is allegedly the real thing. Our Navicarte canal pilot book insists, in a quaint translation, *"it would be sacrilege to leave without tasting the famous Cassoulet"*. This may be so but we have to own up to being sacrilegious. At about £16 a dish we decided to stick with our own recipe ......copies on application!

There are many mooring spots around the south side of the basin and beyond through the road bridge on the old town quay. These are pleasant enough but being alongside public pathways there can sometimes be a problem with unwanted attention. We hit upon a great place to moor at the bottom of the four locks, before entering Castelnaudary. Here, on the port side, there is a wonderfully shaded grassy bank, offering adequate depth, security and tranquillity. The town is only a five-minute walk away and the bonus, which makes the mooring viable for a longer stay, is the fresh water tap we discovered on the wall of a building adjacent to the bottom lock.

Castelnaudry boasts a very large and fine open-air market, selling just about everything. For some time I had been searching for a hat. Not any old hat but a Tilley, a Canadian designed favourite of the yachting fraternity. Hats seem to be popular in Castelnaudry for we came across a couple of enormous comprehensively stocked stalls and there it was, not a genuine Tilley but a pretty good copy. An elderly stallholder was quick to pounce on our interest and we engaged in some good-natured banter explaining why this particular type of hat was special. The deal was eventually done and the hat was not wrapped but worn.

The following day we ascended the four *ecluses de St. Roch*, traversed the basin and worked our way through the built up area to leave the town. It was probably a Sunday as the canal banks were lined with fishermen who generally scowl when a boat passes, no matter how slowly we go. Suddenly there was an agitated shout from one fisherman who was getting very excited about something. "Chapeau, chapeau!!" Of course, we realised, it was the hat seller from the market, who had obviously recognised his sale being worn with pride. We probably made his day and it was a lovely moment.

After Castelnaudry the canal became noticeably quieter. It was a strange sensation but we are sure it's because the tourist trap of Carcassonne lures boaters the other way. A shame really (for them) as there are still many delights, not least reaching the canal summit, the *Col de Naurouze*. This is another legacy of Paul Riquet's triumph at which we marvelled. He designed a maze of feeder canals, pumping stations and reservoirs to ensure an adequate supply of water for the canal, sourced in the Black Mountains. There, in beautiful parkland and perfectly maintained, the system still exists.

From here on it's all downhill to the Atlantic and we found it such a pleasure to be descending after the rise of seventy-three locks. Just after the first lock at the start of this descent, aptly named ecluse de l'Ocean, the canal has an interesting brush with modernity; we were suddenly aware of passing through a motorway service station. The A61 autoroute, accurately named *'between the two seas'*, crosses the canal, and with a visionary piece of planning a fascinating meeting of the old and new has been created. The usual motorway service facilities, that is the usual *French* facilities, set in spacious parkland, have been successfully combined with a canal port and information centre. We discovered the national Rugby museum on the same sight but although this might also be visionary we couldn't quite see it.

The port was busy but it was obvious a number of boats were currently unoccupied. It would be normal procedure to raft alongside a suitable boat for the night and this we and *Gulliver* did, assisted by another couple of cruising Brits, Donna and Mike from *Falcon Crest,* who had squeezed in earlier. A rather fierce lady purporting to be the manager or capitaine descended on us. Rafting alongside was not allowed, *INTERDIT…!* Strange, we thought, and even stranger that the rules were being observed so strictly. We argued and discussed the situation patiently and politely. Jennie, the French language expert did it in French, and Keith did it with charm, one of his virtues. It was all to no avail; Madame would not be moved. Jennie had produced a snack to fortify them as dinnertime was fast approaching. On the verge of defeat she inquired if they could finish it and then move off. Still Madame was unmoved, "you must leave immediately, *maintenant!*" Keith's charm evaporated and as *Gulliver* left the mooring he lifted his not inconsiderable height onto the cabin roof, thanked Donna and Mike for their help and with arms outstretched exclaimed with full Shakespearean drama, **"and you Madam, you are an absolute dragon!!"**

It was not until well into June that we arrived in Toulouse and moored in the middle of the city. Initially it was quite a culture shock. Toulouse however is a very fine city with great shops, great culture, wonderful architecture and everything done with such style and confidence. We even went to a concert! Janet *went to town* and bought an outfit... or two, for a wedding back in Nottingham. All in all we caught up with the consumer society and enjoyed, for a limited period, being in such a vibrant place.

16

...there's someone on the boat

Leaving Toulouse first thing in the morning was an extraordinary experience, literally cruising through the city at rush hour. A modern road system has developed around the three hundred year old canal and carriageways often run parallel on either side. The world around us was at full pelt but we seemed to be in slow motion. At one point the canal crosses a motorway and below us three lanes of jammed traffic.

On the outskirts of the city, in the *port de l'embouchure*, the canal du Midi comes to an end. We passed through a handsomely arched mini tunnel and then into the canal lateral a la Garonne. Opened in 1856 it's a relatively modern construction compared with the canal du Midi and it certainly appears so with improved depth and predictable straightness.

It took some time to leave the extensive suburbs, past a long line of well-established resident barges and then a motorway on one side of the canal and the main railway on the other. This very busy railway line runs parallel with the canal for some thirty kilometres and seems to accommodate almost continuous traffic, night and day. A full day's cruising is necessary to escape the noise but that moment of departure was heaven; birdsong again after city life. We travelled all day in very hot weather but it was worth it to finally moor on the bank-side, just a couple of kilometres before the small town of Montech. Enjoying the wilds of the Montech forest on our starboard side after a couple of weeks in Toulouse, we felt in no mood for a town mooring just yet.

The Canal Lateral, although less hazardous to navigate, is scenically a disappointment after the Midi although admittedly we were spoilt by the constant delight of the older canal. There are moments of agreeable countryside but we were now into arable and fruit country with the wall-to-wall vineyards of Langeudoc a distant happy memory. Boat traffic was sparse. Hire boat bases are few and each holds only a small number of boats, so apart from the odd cruiser or an occasional demasted yacht making the passage from the Atlantic to the Mediterranean the whole atmosphere was agreeably quiet and peaceful.

After a restful night we cruised for all of half an hour to moor in the small but well organised port of Montech. This, we discovered, is the first of a succession of canal side towns that are developing port facilities to encourage tourism. Sadly, and despite their efforts, there were just too few boats. Montech itself is not particularly memorable but it does boast a couple of interesting canal features.

Firstly, the junction with the canal de Montauban, where a ten-kilometre spur should allow us access to that attractive and lively city. Knowing Montauban hosts a major Jazz festival each summer opened up an interesting possibility, particularly as our Jazz singer daughter was due to visit. We were only to find that the spur is currently closed to navigation due to the poor repair of the infrastructure. With such a small amount of traffic we wondered if there would ever be the motivation to invest what was needed.

The second feature, we are able to report, is still working, although mere pleasure boaters are not permitted to use it. It is amazing to think that until quite recently the French government was still investing in the canals, trying to keep them viable for commercial use. As late as the 1970's work was undertaken on the Lateral to enlarge and automate most of the locks and in 1974 the world's first water slope was built to bypass the flight of five locks at Montech. If you have a vessel exceeding 28 metres in length then for a fee you can use this ingenious construction, which moves you, plus the body of water you are floating in, up or down the slope.

The quest to retain commercial traffic on the smaller canals has sadly failed and the water slope is now no more than a tourist attraction, with its main customer a trip boat specifically for this purpose; a strange kind of vicious circle. I'm sure the French government is to be applauded for its valiant effort but perhaps this is one of the weaknesses of today's society; speed and efficiency is everything and the result is an ever-increasing number of trucks on the roads. Who knows, if the canal infrastructure is maintained then a more enlightened time may return. Or am I just an idealist?

As *Starry Vere* is a mere 12.4 metres long we had to do it the hard way and descend the five locks of Montech. Whilst not exactly a 'staircase' they arrive in fairly close succession, each one separated by a lake-like pound. They were never automated or enlarged, the adjacent slope was to take all commercial traffic but a lock keeper overseeing the whole section helps out. However, it seems, he or his wife like to be forewarned of a boat's intention to lock down, understandable with traffic being rather sparse.

The capitaine looking after the port at Montech had, on our arrival, enquired as to when we were moving on but it seems the message didn't reach the eclusier. Our unannounced arrival at the first lock, which is adjacent to his home, was met by a stony face and unabashed disapproval. Perhaps our friend thought he had the afternoon off but we were there and had to be attended to. We did our best to help things along, jumping off the boat and closing lock gates, generally making ourselves available and true, by the end of the flight, he had cheered up somewhat, managing a wave as we left amid our copious *merci beaucoup's!* Perhaps we hadn't reached first name terms but his eclusier's heart had melted… a little.

The canal is virtually dead straight for the ten kilometres to Castelsarrasin but we plumbed for another splendid bank-side mooring four kilometres short of the town, just after the ecluse St. Martin, offering essential shade and depth. The Lateral does generally offer more bank-side depth than the Midi, making spontaneous mooring adventures viable. This is the way we approach our canal cruising, although often leading to many a good cycle ride for provisions.

And on the subject of bicycles... Like most aspiring live-aboards we read vociferously any relevant literature on offer to help our planning but it's not until you are actually doing it that you can usefully evaluate the information these publications contain. Nothing serious, but we were frustrated by one or two pieces of advice we could take issue with. Fold-up bikes for instance. It appears that these are a must, the only ones to have on a boat. Yes, we could see the logic at the time and before leaving the UK we duly purchased a couple of second-hand folders, not the high-tech lightweight specials costing as much as a second hand car, but a couple of heavily built shoppers. These two bikes have certainly earned their keep, one only lasted six months before wearing out, but they have never, ever, been folded! There seems little point as they are in almost daily use, usually along some towpath or country track and there lies the rub. There is no machine worse for negotiating a canal towpath than a folding bike with its miniature wheels. What you need are full size, on-off road, mountain bikes, made for the job, perfect. *We have two beauties sitting in a garage back in the UK!*

From our secluded mooring we cycled along the bank into Castelsarrasin for a spot of shopping and to check out the port facility. By this time Janet is enjoying a 'state of the art' off-roader that Father Christmas delivered from Carrefour, Montpellier. My turn next perhaps. Leaving the tree canopy on the outskirts of town we were struck by the heat of the day and like the majority of the ports on the canal this one is wide open. It was sweltering, so much so that most boat owners had abandoned ship and sought the shade of some nearby trees. We chatted with our fellow boaters and learnt that the exorbitant price of 10 francs per night (about £1) is the charge for mooring, including electricity and all is managed by a very affable and helpful lady called Sylvie, who has a good command of English. It was no wonder some found the place so agreeable that they had put down roots for the summer.

Back at our 'bush mooring' - a wonderfully descriptive name we adopted after meeting a couple of cruising Aussies, Bruce (of course) and Pam, in their boat *Black*

Swan - this seemed like a good time to address a project long in the gestation. Keith and Jennie had moved down to Castelsarrasin to shop, they are not cyclists, and we planned to meet up later. I got the toolbox out. An attractive plank of hard wood, iroko, had been aboard since we left England, earmarked for a much-needed bookcase to fill an empty corner of the saloon. Ship's carpenter set about designing a structure that, by its very nature, consists mainly of right angles. However, in *Starry Vere,* the concept of a right angle just doesn't exist. A challenge but I made a start, although it was to be October before the final coat of varnish was administered.

Despite the lack of shade we eventually decided to move down to the port and enjoy a couple of days in company with friends, old and new. We must have been a bad omen as the weather immediately broke bringing heavy rain just on the day a popular night market was taking place in the town square.

It was still raining when we arrived in the small town of Moissac the following day. There's a good stone walled quay to tie up against and despite the pessimism of our canal guide, the English translation calls it, *"an apparently innocuous town"*, *anodine* in the original French, we felt Moissac has at least as much to offer as Castelsarrasin and infinitely more than Montech. The large Saturday morning market was certainly one of the best we had found and the Abbey Church of St. Peter is a magnificent concealed treasure. Perhaps some local politics going on here but I've done my bit to right the wrongs of Moissac. We cruised straight through Valence D'Agen, disappointed with what we saw, although our appreciation would be updated on the return leg and as we entered the large canal basin at

Agen we spotted *Gulliver* moored alongside the grassy bank.

Agen is described as the *"pearl of the midi"* and whilst I don't make a habit of being at odds with our guide book, Janet and I certainly didn't warm to the place. Perhaps if you are a prune devotee then your heart rate might rise, for this is the prune centre of the world. Each September a 'fete de la prune' takes place or, for year round satisfaction, there's always the prune museum. Needless to say the shops are full of more varieties of this delicacy than one could ever image but unfortunately we are not very keen. As Janet pointed out, our diet is rich in museli, bran and bananas so we have that base covered, so to speak.

Perhaps the city fathers' exertions in selling the prune have distracted them from providing adequate canal side facilities, they are certainly lacking - that's the facilities. There is a port de plaisance but this is no more than a small hire boat base situated adjacent to a very main road. For a large city, with plenty of canal side space, it's somewhat mystifying. Leaving Agen, which we did quite promptly, the canal is transported over the Garonne river by a spectacular five hundred and thirty nine metre long prune…no …aqueduct!

It may sound trivial to say so but we found the long stretch from Agen to Buzet a little dull. The canal is straight with quite high banks at times that restricted our view. Keith, in *Gulliver* up front and I played a game of bird watching by VHF radio. Kingfishers in particular were wonderfully numerous, I saw more in a day than I've seen in total before.

The main bonus when reaching the small but characterful village of Buzet is a visit to the splendid cave co-operative. The wine of Buzet was once more important than Bordeaux and after a period of decline it is now thriving and delicious. The cave is certainly geared up to sell, with prices higher than we found in Langoudoc but after an extensive degustation we chose a few bottles that appealed to us.

It's here that the option becomes available to lock down onto two rivers, the Baïse and the Lot. It seemed like an interesting diversion and although the Navicarte pilot book gives an available depth of 1.5 metres up to the town of Lavardac and a mere 1 metre through Nerac and Condom, we had suffered a fair few days of rain that could make an enormous difference to levels. Locking down the twin locks onto the Baïse was a terribly slow process, we never really found out why and although the machinery appeared to have been automated it seemed to operate at a very slow pace. The trip down from canal to river was a popular option for the hire boats leaving the base at Buzet so invariably there was a bottleneck at the lock. Once we were down a sharp right turn took us into the Baïse and into a very different atmosphere. The change was quite dramatic with undergrowth encroaching well into the brown water, along with fallen trees, the odd large rock, oh, and the *occasional* hire boat appearing out of the undergrowth. The weather too was odd, almost a microclimate with an overcast sky and intermittent drizzle reminding us of holidaying in Scotland!

Up to the first lock and mooring at Vianne presented no problems. A very pleasant spot, with a good quay, electricity and water freely available and a fascinating walled 'town' (really only a village) complete with 12th century church. Next day, acting on a tip from a friendly hire boat crew who were on their way back downstream, we decide to bypass the next moorings at Lavardac and head for Nerac, which is reputed to be the most beautiful town on the river. The banks remained heavily wooded with many trees either in the water or leaning precariously. Concentration on the helm was paramount but it is very difficult to legislate for what is going on beneath the surface, even with various bits of technology flashing away.

Our serene progress eventually 'ground' to a halt as we approached the ecluse St Crabary. We wondered why the current was not carrying us back as we waited for *Gulliver* to lock through before us. Attempting to move forward all was revealed, the bottom had come up to meet us. Not a soft muddy bottom either but something hard and aggressive. We gave it a couple of attempts but the nasty sound of steel against, at best, gravel soon persuaded us our progress up the Baïse was over. We made a safe about-turn to Lavardac with no damage sustained and contented ourselves with a visit to the excellent Super U supermarket on the outskirts of town. *Gulliver* has a far shallower draught than *Starry Vere* and was able to safely reach Nerac. It was Jennie's birthday, we had brought a present, so determined not to be thwarted we cycled into Nerac for the celebration. Wandering around the small town it certainly is a gem of a place.

Apart from the supermarket there was nothing to detain us at Lavardac and as the important French holiday celebrating the fall of the Bastille on July 14 was fast approaching we thought we would move back down to Vianne and let the weekend pass peacefully. Most communities celebrate this day with gusto and all invariably ends with a firework display of some description. For some reason Vianne's celebration seemed to be low key. There was a night market the evening before, which included a great deal of eating and drinking. Virtually the entire network of streets around the central square had been laid out with tables and chairs and an open-air bar established appearing to only sell the local wine, and then only by the bottle! Anyway this was all happening a fair walk from the river so we had no worries about being disturbed.

Our mooring was on Vianne's old stone quay, situated immediately above a weir with the remains of a large mill that at one time would have been a hive of activity. On average about six boats can moor on the quay and this evening it was completely full with *Starry Vere* at the head of the quay, furthest from the weir. We noticed a firework display in some distant community as we turned in but our expectation was of another untroubled night.

Janet disturbed first, just before midnight. With a dig in the ribs I was brought to a state of near consciousness to hear a nervous whisper, "there's someone on the boat". The quay has no artificial light and it was very dark when we gingerly peered out from behind the curtains. A couple of shadowy figures, now off the boat, seemed to be huddled around an electricity and water point housed in a substantial stone structure, so substantial that a mooring rope from our stern had been tied around it. Putting to one side the thought that we may have had intruders on board my initial reaction was perhaps some other boat owner may be attending to an electric or water problem. Anyway, **WE** decided it prudent to investigate and **I** pulled on some clothes and made my way out of the boat. By this time the two figures had made off down the length of the quay and could just be distinguished, again huddled over something. Then I made the disturbing discovery; our stern rope had been completely severed. OK this was serious but what best to do? The culprits were probably still up to no good but they obviously had a knife or two, which is a sobering thought in the dead of night. Our French neighbour stirred and climbed out of his small cruiser. We shared a general moan as I attempted to make good our stern mooring rope. The movement on the quay must have alerted the intruders and the next thing we knew they were making a hasty retreat into the darkness on a couple of mopeds. The Frenchman wandered down the quay to see what was what but amazingly no one else stirred. It was an unnerving experience and I preferred to 'stand guard' looking out into the shadows for some time before feeling happy about attempting sleep again.

The morning arrived and the knot in our rope confirmed it hadn't all been a bad dream. Our neighbour surfaced and we had a further moan as we walked down the quay. We came across a phenomenon that is still baffling. Immediately above the weir a small hired cabin cruiser had moored with a Dutch couple on board, enjoying the first night of their holiday. They were up and about and although having climbed off the boat to walk up to the village to buy bread, what they hadn't noticed was that both of their mooring ropes had also been completely severed. There was absolutely nothing holding that boat to the quay for most of the night, yet it didn't move. What's more, the idiots responsible had also cut the very thick rope stretching across the river immediately above the weir, a boom placed there to prevent any drifting boats from going over. Why the boat hadn't moved we could not fathom but two lucky people slept peacefully, unaware of the potential danger.

The Dutchman and I decided that such was the seriousness of the incident we should walk up to the

Mairie and let someone know. We began to explain in our halting French to the receptionist what had transpired but quite by chance the Mayor himself appeared and when he grasped the seriousness of our complaint he took over the case. Of course the incident was potentially life threatening, but the small communities alongside the river depend a great deal on seasonal tourism from boaters and the Mayor could already see the newspaper headlines. He had no English but we gave him the whole story as best we could and immediately a call was put through to the local Gendarmarie, who, we were informed, would arrive at some point. Back down on the quay the Dutch couple, valuing their holiday and wary about getting involved in any protracted bureaucracy, decided to leave. We were in no hurry and so agreed to relay the happenings to the authorities when they arrived on the scene.

It wasn't long before an official cavalcade drew up at the port, not just the Gendarme in blue police car but also the Mayor in his smart four-wheel drive and a French waterways representative, the VNF, in a not so smart white van. We were getting the full treatment but I was glad they were taking it seriously. The official group of four marched up the quay toward us and just within earshot the Mayor turned to his colleagues to enquire, *"parlez vous anglais?"* The answer seemed to be a definite no and the Mayor, being the senior partner, was propelled forward to deal with *les anglais.* By now I had rehearsed the facts of the story so many times that my French was getting quite creditable, well at least they seemed to understand. The knot in our rope was thoroughly examined with sympathetic tutting and disapproving intakes of breath but whether the culprits were ever apprehended, we'll never know. The incident proved to be

162

a disappointing dent in our excellent impression of French social behaviour. We realise there must be crime and social problems but our experience in both town and country had been pleasantly worry and trouble free.

So much for our Baïse adventure. We certainly didn't think it wise to tackle the adjoining River Lot so it was a return to the relative reliability of the canal and on toward Bordeaux.

17

...personal service at its zenith

Cruising through the waterways of France we have experienced our fair share of surprises. Apart from the odd bit of vandalism with our mooring ropes most have been pleasant but discovering an original and quite brilliant artistic masterpiece, not a five-minute walk from the canal, was certainly a highlight.

We arrived at the canal-side village of Le Mas d'Agenais, yet another small but attractive community, steeped in history as most are. It has a number of lovely buildings and a tremendous open-sided wooden beamed market hall, which normally would be the focus of attention for any visitor. It also has a Romanesque 12th century church which we found masked by scaffolding and plastic sheeting, so much so that we could quite easily have been dissuaded from making the effort to investigate.

Walking into the church there is no hint of the treasure it contains, all looks very similar to a hundred other French churches into which we have escaped for a cool half an hour. In a small side chapel we noticed some wooden steps leading up to a platform and on the wall a large glass fronted case. The lighting is very dim but a simple and certainly aged notice, just to one side, announces that the case houses an original Rembrant painting, one in a series of religious tableau the great artist painted concerned with the crucifixion of Christ. The notice also informed us that if a *jeton* was purchased and deposited in the slot of a box looking not dissimilar to a gas meter, the painting would be illuminated for a few minutes with a recorded commentary, in English if we desired. We certainly desired a *jeton* and from a list of outlets in the village the only one we could find open was the local bar. It was all so low key, even primitive but we hurried back to a deserted church for our private viewing. The 10-franc *jeton* was posted in the slot, the lights came on and there, before just the two of us, was the staggeringly beautiful painting of Jesus crucified on the cross. Even as religious doubters we could not fail to be moved by the way Rembrant had captured the agony of the moment, the scale of the grief.

The accompanying commentary informed us that the painting had been purchased at an auction a century or more before by a family who originated from Mas D'Argenais but who had moved to the northern town of Dunkirk. The picture was presented to the church as a gift and in obscurity there it hung for many years. Subsequently a later incumbent parish priest, oblivious of its origin, plotted to sell the picture to raise money for essential church repairs. It was delivered to Paris for valuation and it was only then that the artist was identified and its importance revealed. Strangely the painting wasn't sold, although the remaining five tableaux in the series hang in a German gallery. One can speculate on the heart searching this must have caused, for it would be hard to imagine the gallery not wishing to reunite the lost painting with the set. Yet, in the Church of St. Vincent, in splendid isolation, the painting still hangs. On the face of it with only modest protection although I would like to think that the security is more sophisticated than it appears. We were able to mount the steps leading up onto the viewing platform and experience the rare pleasure of very close contact; just a sheet of protective glass between us and such a great painting. We marvelled at the way every brush stroke was clearly visible. To see so closely how the painting had been created, particularly with its difficult and painful subject, made for a most awe-inspiring experience.

The excellent new bank-side facility at Pont des Sables is as near as we could get to the city of Marmande, a good six kilometres down the main road that passes over a nearby bridge, the *pont des Sables* I presume. We were in need of provisions and investigated an ancient looking local general store near the mooring. Walking in we were struck by the sheer untidiness; tins, packets, magazines, bits of hardware, all piled high, the shop probably sold most things anyone would need if you could ever find them. A comparison with our daughter's bedroom in her teenage years came to mind, but the shop probably had the edge. The impressive display of fruit and vegetables caught our eye; they appeared as ancient as the building. Obviously the sell by date system had not reached this establishment. Janet tentatively picked up a tomato for closer inspection and was horrified by a swarm of little flies and mites she had disturbed. Perhaps the racks were refilled when the old stock walked out, or more likely, *crawled out,* under its own steam! We made a quick exit; I don't think I could even be persuaded to buy a newspaper from the place. But we still needed provisions and there must be a supermarket in Marmande. Six kilometres each way or starve. No contest, the cycle ride won the day.

It seemed to be the time for long cycle rides. We had been reading in a superb book by Hilary Wright, *Water into Wine,* about the considerable merits of the local Côtes du Marmandais. A little further up the canal we read, was a good departure point for reaching the village of Cocument where we would find the cave co-operative producing a particularly good example of this local brew. Just past the *ecluse de Bernes* we secured to a suitable bank side mooring and evidently the road crossing the canal just near the lock was the one to follow. The weather was a little changeable, there was even a hint of rain but that wouldn't deter us. What did make us think twice about the expedition was that the seven kilometres from the canal to Cocument are a continuous, inexorable, exhausting incline! Oh Hilary, you failed to tell us about the hill. The D3 climbs steadily out of the Garonne valley with the wine cave, on the outskirts of Cocument, virtually on the summit. It took a supreme act of faith in Ms Wright's judgement to keep us at it. To be truthful it was worth the effort just for the wonderful vista of the Garonne valley. The wine was as we were told it would be and of course descending back down to the canal, with rucksacks heavily laden, was a cyclists dream; no peddling.

We had visitors on their way, Pat and Tony from the UK and we had to locate a suitable and agreeable spot in which to rendezvous. They also needed a safe haven for their new car, which turned out to be a very flash bright red sporty number, just the thing for secreting away on the canal bank. The superb mooring at Meilhan, just a further day's cruising above Marmande, turned out to be perfect for our need. This was probably the most delightful mooring on the canal, the kind of spot we could quite happily spend a longer period of time enjoying. The canal opens out into a small pound with a modest but very attractive port, adjacent to a surprisingly attractive campsite. The mooring was excellent, against a concrete wall with electricity and water all available. Both camping and port are administered from a small bar that also served as a tourist information centre with staff friendly and helpful. However, important though these attributes are, it is the setting that makes it such a pleasant place. No more than a hundred metres away off our starboard side, is the broad expanse of the Garonne River. Probably quite treacherous in the winter but now, in late July, it was shallow and benign, ideal for a cooling paddle. On our port side, as we sat on the quayside facing west, the terrain climbs very steeply up to the village of Meilhan which is situated at this much higher level. So, the bad news is that to buy the bread each morning means an energetic, heart-pumping climb up to the village. The good news, and there's plenty of that, is the village itself which is a delight. It has a most unique feature, an amazing viewpoint, the *site du Tertre,* which looks out over the Garonne valley to Marmande in the far distance. The viewpoint has recently been beautifully developed and now serves as a kind of communal square, albeit on the edge of the village. It's an impressive open space used for a wide variety of events. Whilst we were in town a *fete de Livre* was held, a book fair, and the space was full of stalls offering a variety of books and book related goods. It was definitely a cultural event and a mini theatre had been erected to accommodate a series of dramatic performances. Naturally, there was also a great deal of *al fresco* eating taking place including a grand communal meal.

Whilst on the subject of eating, we discovered that Meilhan has quite probably the best *boucherie* you are ever likely to come across in France. It is housed in a smart yet unassuming shop but on entering what becomes immediately apparent is that this establishment takes its role very seriously. In butchery terms this is hallowed ground. On the wall is proudly posted the source of all the meat currently available for purchase and of course this means local producers. Behind the scenes work a number of butchers preparing meat for the counter. In the shop itself, at the high altar, only one man serves, perhaps the proprietor, meaning personal service at its zenith. A second person stands in the shadow of a corner to deal with the necessary evil of payment. Bearing in mind the shop is very popular at all hours you can imagine the queues. It must be one of the few butchers worldwide where seating is provided! Needless to say, we patronised the shop a number of times, the meat was superb but we also enjoyed just observing what and in what quantities meat was being purchased. We suspected the concept of vegetarianism was alien to the French but never more so than among the carnivores of Meilhan sur Garonne.

During a friendly event organised to welcome boaters and campers to the village I met the mayor who speaks perfect English. He was mingling with the crowd furnishing a bottle of Scotch for those who fancied a nip. His intention to keep Meilhan vibrant and viable was certainly succeeding, perhaps he should also add well fed!

With the arrival of visitors imminent we had to focus our minds on what we were actually going to do. The end of the canal at Castets en Dorthe is only eighteen kilometres further on. From there stretches over fifty kilometres of Garonne estuary, tidal and gradually becoming a major seaway, before reaching our original goal of Bordeaux. It was a dilemma we toyed with but finally common sense prevailed. Pat and Tony were probably all set to enjoy a relaxing few days of their summer holiday in the South of France. Their expectation we felt sure would be of a leisurely, stress free cruise and we know full well they enjoy the delights of eating and drinking. No, the estuary was unknown territory to us and to be fair we had heard negative reports from friends who had ventured down to Bordeaux and regretted it. We would forsake salt water for the moment and cruise the canal back to Buzet where we could all enjoy the fruits of the cave co-operative. It was a sensible decision and all went very well; five days of leisurely eating and drinking plus a little relaxed cruising and the weather was perfect. We resigned ourselves to Bordeaux just not being possible, which was disappointing. For the future though I had already lodged away the idea that if and when we return to the UK we could do it via the canals, into the Garonne estuary calling at Bordeaux, and then up the Brittany coast to the English Channel.

18

...it's all true, I was there

As so often seemed to be happening we were faced with another deadline, although for very pleasant reasons. Emma and Adam were visiting again, flying into Carcassonne and my sister Gail plus partner, Roy, who were holidaying in France, had planned to meet us for a day. The family gathering had been arranged for Valance D'Agen, easily accessible by road and train but intriguingly we had been tipped off about a happening in Valance that shouldn't be missed.

Once Pat and Tony had departed, the red sporty number packed to the roof with *vin de la region*, we left Meilhan directly and moored for the final time at Buzet, the bush mooring again, under the trees, which for once was not a good idea. We endured a disturbed night caused by a nasty yet rather impressive summer storm. Thunder, spectacular lightning and rain, so torrential that most of the sticky slimy leaf canopy of the high summer Plane trees deposited itself all over the boat in the form of a gluttonous green grunge. The new day brought sunshine again that for once was not welcome as the heat looked set to weld this disgusting substance into a permanent new surface. For a couple of hours we washed and scrubbed before finding white paint and teak decks again.

A further day and a half cruising and we arrived in Valance. Just before the port the canal passes under an innocuous road bridge; we passed under and emerged into no less than a theatrical auditorium! On our starboard side was a village that certainly wasn't there when we passed through earlier in the month. A double take and we realised it was a stage set, a full size village facade, complete with church, stretching some hundred metres down the canal bank. Over on our port side, directly opposite, a bank of tiered seating, an enormous construction capable of accommodating thousands of people without doubt. And there, beautifully situated with a grandstand view of the whole scene, were the pontoons of the port. Stuart and Jackie greeted us on *Kiama*, the source of our tip-off via the wonders of e-mail, the perfect medium for the cruising life. They were well positioned alongside with a couple of other boats but there was adequate room for *Starry Vere* to settle in and await our visitors and the forthcoming spectacle.

But what on earth had we sailed into? It was certainly a theatrical event and looking at the seating a large audience was expected. During the following days it was fascinating to sit in our prime spot and observe the activity. We were subjected to various sound checks from the enormous banks of speakers and tantalising mini rehearsals by individuals going through their cameo scenes; tension was visibly rising. One evening, as darkness fell, the lighting and sound technicians launched into a full rehearsal giving a first glimpse of what was unfolding before us. It was stunning but there was more to come as it proved to be dress rehearsal night; now we could really begin to get a feel of what this was all about. We sat on the back of the boat spellbound, mesmerised, barely believing our luck at being in this place at just the right time.

It is called *Au fil de l'eau*, an annually produced show that, through tracing the lives of three characters, Lucien, Theodore and Guillaume, as they move from schooldays into adulthood, charts the history of Valence over the past hundred years. This journey has been realised from the collective memory of the community who are represented by over three hundred local people acting as themselves. The scenery is life sized, the costumes are authentic. There are live animals, a museum's worth of period vehicles, barges coming and going on the canal, which, as it would have been years ago is central to the story. There are moments of humour, of romance, and moments of drama such as the re-enactment of the German occupation in World War II. In particular the moment when, after the death of one German soldier in the town, a large number of local men were executed as an act of revenge. This distressing incident is chillingly portrayed and although it has been subject to criticism over the years, particularly from the inevitable German tourists, the people of Valance have insisted that as a true and dark moment in their history it has to be retained. Our Canadian neighbour in the port relayed to us his poignant experience the previous year when sitting amongst the audience. This difficult part of the story reached, an elderly lady next to him turned and said, "it's all true, I was there".

Our family visitors arrived on the day of the first performance and were no doubt a little bemused by our obvious excitement. Ten o'clock in the evening all was revealed and along with many hundreds of people packing the rows of seats in the stands we, in our *royal box*, were absolutely enchanted by what we experienced.

We had two weeks to enjoy Emma and Adam's company aboard before delivering them back to Carcassonne for the flight home. Just enough time for a little leisurely sight seeing but we would need to travel almost every day. Back through Moissac, Castelsarrasin, Montech, the beauty of retracing our steps is that we have done the groundwork and can appear well-informed hosts. It was after Montech, on the long straight stretch back toward Toulouse, that the starboard engine raw water pump started causing problems. This is the pump that circulates seawater, or in our current situation canal water, through a heat exchanger to cool the engine's cooling water, a boat equivalent of the radiator. Anyway, when the pump decides to give up the result is an overheating engine. We continued for a while on one engine, only a potential problem if manoeuvring in a confined space, until we reached the simple mooring near the village of Grisolles where I attempted a repair. Unfortunately, although a pleasant enough spot, the canal from here to Toulouse runs adjacent to the main railway with its relentless traffic, night and day. Laying in our bunk at an otherwise very quite spot a train would first be heard approaching in the far distance. Getting ever closer it climaxed as if passing right through the boat and then in the darkness it rumbled off into the night before the distant sound of the next one approaching kept us from sleep. A good incentive to fix the pump but easier said than done. These pumps had seen their best days, I had already rebuilt them on a number of occasions and it was difficult to get the necessary seals and bearings, downright impossible in canal-side Grisolles.

I got it working in a fashion, re-fitted it and we made haste off down the canal hoping to reach Toulouse. The pump didn't last long and so we were back down to one engine making the narrow confines of the canal entering the city somewhat tricky. We only had one minor altercation with a stone-walled bank side before making fast with some relief in the city centre port. It's at times like this that Derek Bowskill's little gem comes to mind, *"boats is bover"* but at least Emma and Adam, with Janet as guide, could take off and enjoy the city whilst I searched metric Toulouse for a supplier of imperial sized bearings.

Very close to the port is the headquarters of the *Sapeur Pompier*, the fire station. I reckoned they would be helpful kind of people and should know the city well. I took the old bearing along as a visual aid to supplement my French! It did the trick and a very helpful and patient sapeur, if that's the correct terminology, guided me to exactly the establishment I needed. There was a drawback, it was a little out of town, but what's a good cycle ride through the busy streets of one of belle France's more major cities. The reward for my efforts was to be greeted by an English speaker who made life much easier. They could even get hold of the bearing I needed but not for at least 24 hours. Still, no complaints and looking at it positively I now knew the route through the busy suburbs of Toulouse.

With pump rebuilt - again - and an ample dose of retail therapy enjoyed we departed the city and returned to the pastoral idyll of the canal, with two engines in action. A night in Montgiscard and then an early start plus a full day brought us back to one of our favourite bank-side moorings at Castelnaudary. We could only afford a morning showing Emma and Adam the sights of cassoulet town as our mechanical problems had made the schedule even tighter. The final stop before Carcassonne was at the wooden pontoon mooring of Villepinte. This time the ancient washer-women were absent but we met an equally ancient fisherman who had planted himself in the middle of the pontoon against which we were aiming to moor. It was a squeeze but we tried hard not to disturb him, in any case he carried on seemingly oblivious of our arrival. Like the washer-folk we met on our way up, this fisherman looked as though he had been sitting in the same position for a hundred years.

Come the morning he was there again. We felt sure he must have gone home overnight but no, he was there in the same spot as though he had never been away. We needed another early start so by nine the engines were running and we cast off the ropes to leave the pontoon. Emma and Adam were still in their bunks as we left the bank-side, a friendly wave to the ancient fisherman but no response. Within seconds a routine peaceful departure had turned into a disaster. Two events transpired to create this unfortunate start to the day. Firstly the previous evening I had returned our smaller mast on the front deck to the upright position to make more room for al fresco dining. Secondly, we left the mooring without lowering it again; I was probably guilty of paying too much attention to the fisherman. But there is also a third and crucial part to this tale of woe, a mere twenty metres on is a bridge, a typical low steel girdered canal bridge…

We must have been no more than two metres away when I realised. It was too late but instinctively I rammed the boat into reverse and gave it full throttle, what could be called an emergency stop. With an horrendous crack the top of the mast struck the bridge. The glass anchor light shattered into many pieces and my beautiful varnished teak flexed, bowed and then splintered. Reverse propulsion took effect and we started to come back out from under the bridge with the mast scraping along the underneath of the steel girders, doubling the carnage, if that were possible. The sudden burst of full throttle also had the effect of clearing out a summer's exhaust grunge accumulated by slow running. In a second we were engulfed in our own personal smoke screen. Emma and Adam, in nightgown and boxer shorts respectively, scrambled out onto the deck thinking it was their last moment. Not only had they been woken by a great crash immediately above their heads, their cabin had filled with exhaust smoke as the boat, still in reverse, passed back through the cloud. I peered over through the mist to see a group of fishermen on the bank transfixed by the Armageddon they had witnessed, breaking into the peace of a lovely morning. Sad and ashamed as I am to admit it but this was not the first time I had attempted to bend the mast double. There had been a similar lapse back on the River Trent and like then I now had to rebuild it, piece by piece.

19

...the sea, "the endless sea"

We reached our goal of Carcassonne with just one day to spare, time enough for Emma and Adam to explore the old cité and for us all to enjoy a repeat of our wedding anniversary *al fresco* lunch in the lovely square. Then, sadly, they departed and we were two again. Our hectic spell of entertaining now over Janet and I could begin to concentrate on the remainder of the canal taking us to our exit into the sea. After a summer's detour, albeit highly enjoyable, our original quest of entering the Mediterranean beckoned; it was time to complete the first part of our master plan. Well it would have been but no sooner had Emma and Adam left then Janet took to her sick bed with some kind of bug that laid her low. The weather reflected the general malaise and we spent three more doleful days in Carcassone with the wind blowing hard, heavy showers dampening the spirits of the many tourists in town and Janet flat on her back. My penance was to begin the job of rebuilding the mast.

With tender love and care Janet began to recover, which was more than could be said for the mast, although my 'TLC' had been equally dispensed. We could at last leave Carcassonne and head for just after le Somail, where the canal divides. Our plan was to leave the Midi at this point and take the *canal de Jonction* to Narbonne, then, via the *canal de la Robine*, we would enter the sea.

Wind, rain and fever abated allowing us to reach our all time favourite mooring at Puicheric and then twenty-four hours later we moored alongside a grassy bank at Roubia, with a mission.

On our way up the canal, some three months earlier, we had moored at the same spot alongside *Gulliver*. With the 'ringing' recommendation of Hilary Wright we had set out on the not inconsiderable cycle ride to find Chateau de Fontareche, "less than three kilometres away, on the Lezignan road", was the assurance we read. It was a wonderful day and the ride through the very extensive vineyards of the Corbieres was to be fair no hardship, particularly when the expert says this is the best visit on the canal. It just has to be done.

On arrival the instructions were to ring the bell marked *'vente de vin'* and I quote, "we would soon find ourselves in an interesting if dark tasting cellar".

We rang the bell, warm from our exertions but pleasantly apprehensive. We rang it again, then again, louder but with no response. As we had turned off the main road into the estate we noticed a group of folk playing Boule. Wearily pushing our bikes back we enquired if they could shed any light on our problem. Of course they could, it was a *jour de fete*, a public holiday, that's why they were playing Boule and not responding to the ringing bell! We withdrew gracefully and cycled back dejected but not defeated.

Now we had returned, determined to test out Ms Wright's recommendation. This time ringing the bell with success, we were invited into the "interesting yet dark tasting cellar". Our host was charming, our degustation thorough and the wine absolutely excellent but of course we were faced with the same dilemma; transporting the goodies. We did our best and staggered back to the canal with half a dozen bottles each, packed into our rucksacks.

Another day's gentle and relaxed cruising and we moored where the aptly named *canal de jonction* leaves the Midi and drops down through seven closely spaced locks to the level of the River Aude. A short stretch of the river has to be crossed to reach the entrance to the *canal de la Robine*. We had arrived at lunchtime and as all closes at this sacred time of day we moored alongside and enjoyed our lunch, looking forward to moving into new territory.

Lunchtime over we approached the first lock, no more than a hundred metres after leaving the Midi. We were met by the lady eclusiére who assailed us in French that was not immediately grasped but the general line was something like "where do you think you're going?" We hoped to reach Narbonne, we explained but it was not to be. The eclusiére had our best interests at heart for it transpired the water level in the Aude was so low we would be in danger of running aground, a problem quite common in the dry summer months.

So our exit from the canals was going to take a little longer than expected and we would have to continue retracing our steps down the Midi, all the way back to Agde, before the next opportunity to reach the ocean. It was still August and apart from the danger of falling water levels, the hire boats were out in force. Although it was not a prospect that filled me with delight, our options were somewhat limited; perhaps best to think positively and enjoy a second opportunity to savour the beauty of the canal.

The Foncerannes locks had to be negotiated once more but descending is a far less daunting prospect than ascending. The times each day when boats can ascend or descend are strictly regulated. Descending has a slot first thing each morning and although we made an early start we were staggered to see just how many boats were juggling for position to enter the top lock. Four boats at a time are squeezed into the chamber by a team of eclusiers keen to get the job done and as the majority of boats are hire craft, we lingered at the top and chose our partners carefully.

The port at Beziers was the ideal spot to spend a few days finishing the mast repair and attending to a few other chores in preparation for returning to the salt. Below Beziers we very cautiously edged our way past the notorious submerged car spot as a second encounter was not what we wanted at this stage. We were struck by the difference in the countryside around the canal. The previous April and May it had been lush and green but now the hot summer had taken its toll and all was brown and quite barren in places. The water too had changed its hue, perhaps 'matured' would be a good description, into a most uninviting green soup.

And so with August almost spent we arrived back at the stone quay, just above the round lock of Agde. Our canal adventure was almost at an end but the sea would offer many challenges, that's for sure. We had left Farndon on the River Trent fourteen months earlier with an aim of reaching the Mediterranean and our goal was now very close.

I also had another target, more tenuous, more elusive and probably more important. Quite simply it was for us both to be content and happy. Bitterness is a very destructive state of mind, one that I know achieves nothing. The cause of such a negative state has to be dealt with, worked through and contextualised. Time does heal, in the sense that feelings and emotions concerned with loss and indeed bitterness do become numbed. But to have remained in the same environment would have meant just that, a numbing, a local anaesthetic rather than a full cure. I set out on a search for reconciliation. Firstly I had to make my peace with the very art form that had been at the centre of everything. Gradually, very gradually, as we journeyed through new scenes and new experiences, I began to listen to music again with enjoyment, divorcing it from the emotional baggage into which it had become entwined. But most of all I have had the space to recognise the true nature of life. It is amazing how space and time was needed to begin to appreciate and learn from what I had held in awe for years. Mellville's tale of Billy Budd, magnified through Britten's great opera, teaches us that natural goodness, natural evil and human justice each play their part and how we are at their mercy. It is man's role to arbitrate, to interpret. This is the tragedy that is embodied in Captain Vere, Starry Vere, and his ship *Indomitable.* And so I have been able to put to rest my loss. To place it in some kind of context that will not cloud other parts of my life, those past and those still to come. Without a doubt, if I had embarked on this voyage before launching into enormous and ambitious projects, such as forming a professional orchestra, all would have been different. It comes down to education. Our fourteen-month voyage so far has been an enlightening, a widening, a growing process. I can now understand why for instance in the 19th century, so many privileged young people were sent on the grand tour around Europe. Admittedly a very different Europe but the gain is the same with or without the EU or the Euro. Experiencing and coping with language, tradition and culture, is life enriching, essential for any artist whose working medium is life itself. But no matter, I now look forward. Yes there are still moments of sadness but with less bitterness. Our voyage has taught me how to be excited again, for without excitement there is no life.

*

The plan was to lock through onto the Herault river in the early evening, find a riverside mooring for the night and then have the advantage of an early start for our first Mediterranean voyage across the Gulf de Lyon to Port Vendres, the penultimate port before the Spanish border. We met up again with friends Ted and Sue who have lived in Agde on their brilliantly self-built yacht 'Moston Dragon' for some time. We discovered that Paul and Fearne in 'Force Five' had set up camp for the summer just the other side of the lock on the river and it was as we were cycling back from saying our hellos and goodbyes that we discovered a traffic jam at the lock. There had been a robbery... so I overheard in a discussion between a couple of locals. Certainly our passage through the lock was going to be impeded because a team of divers from the Gendarmerie was searching for something and all boat traffic was at a halt. It appeared that a robbery had occurred at the Post office of a nearby village and the fleeing robbers had thrown some of their booty, the evidence, into the lock. I don't suppose their getaway vehicle was a boat, not even a speedy hire boat, but with the main road passing over the canal adjacent to the lock, it seemed feasible. Our departure from the canal was eventually postponed, the agony prolonged, but it gave us time for just one more drink with friends in Agde.

Nine o'clock the following morning and we entered the lock to descend onto the River Herault. Paul and Fearne had made a wonderful gesture, rising particularly early to see us off! It was a beautiful morning, blue sky and crucially very little wind. The short canal link from the lock took us to the main river and once under the road bridge we could make our last alteration to take us from canal cruisers to sea goers. Up went the refurbished front mast, newly applied varnish reflecting in the brilliant early morning sun. Then the larger rear mast with radar and VHF aerials, erect again for the first time in a year. Nervous checks of the instruments; oil pressure, temperature. Listening to the sound of the engines, already turning faster than on the canals. Under the high motorway bridge. Past the fishing boats and fish freezing plant on our port side. Past the familiar scene of Allemandes boatyard and then there it is, the sea, no fuss, no interruption, the river melting away into the vast expanse of dark blue water and a massive deep blue sky.

The end of the stone training wall passed behind us, Janet standing close squeezed my arm and smiled, that was enough. We had to pick our way through a myriad of small fishing boats immobile on a glassy calm surface, two or three figures in each boat becalmed with intent concentration on rod and line. They didn't give *Starry Vere* a second glance as we passed into the sea, the *"endless sea"*.

Postlude

'From Mozart to the Med' has spent a number of years languishing on a hard disk. I occasionally tinkered with it but life moved on at such a pace there was always the new adventure to occupy me. Finally I have got it out of my system and for better or for worse, published!

It was a great moment for us to enter the Mediterranean, to achieve what we set out to do and we did enjoy a year cruising down some of the Spanish coast, plus a couple of the Balearic Islands. We were in Barcelona on 9/11 (2001) and will never forget the sombre atmosphere we woke up to that grim morning, particularly as the port contained many yachts from the US. A winter in Tarragona gave us the opportunity to mix and mingle with Spanish society and although we enjoyed a sunny Christmas it was a strange winter with snowstorms, evidently the first for forty years and massive seas breaking over the sea wall. The unpredictability of the weather was in fact the catalyst sending us back to the inland waterways of France. The romantic notion of an idyllic flat blue sea was just that, a romantic notion. For most of the time we rocked and rolled and on occasion we could have been sheltering from the worst of the North Atlantic. We decided to sell *Starry Vere*, a decision mixed with emotion and practical sense. She had looked after us so well during our learning curve but now the vagaries of sea, salt and the southern sun were making her a very high maintenance proposition.

And what did we buy?

Even more work, a classic 28 metre Dutch barge, The Anthonia.

And where are we now?

Still afloat... as I write peacefully moored alongside the stone quay of a small village on one of the beautiful canals of Burgundy. The Anthonia is a marvellous home; spacious, comfortable and characterful and if we feel like a change of scenery, we just untie the ropes and move on!

It's a great life-style and we now enjoy sharing it with guests.

Check us out on :-
www.bargeanthonia.com
or
www.bargeholidaysfrance.com

a bientôt

Printed in the United Kingdom
by Lightning Source UK Ltd.
132178UK00001B/384/P